Advance Praise for ~~Start Line and~~

A great reminder to us all of the power of positive thinking, the strength of family and the magic of setting goals and chasing them. What I love most about this book is that this could be you, your next door neighbor, your family member. Challenges in life face us all, but so do the wonders of competitive sports and teamwork. Dr. Asp's story is inspirational and proof that belief and hard work can conquer all!
Jessie Diggins
U.S.A. Olympic Team Cross Country Skier
Elite Level Skier in World Cup and World Championship

This is a powerfully wonderful journey through some of the emotions and trails of life with a focus on faith, hope, resilience and rising above life's daunting challenges. Dr. Asp does a masterful job…this book exude positive emotions, focusing on the ability to improve one's self with empowerment, grit and reliance on a higher power. This is truly an amazing journey that has the power to uplift any reader.
Jerry Brewer M.D.

From the physical and mental challenge of athletic competition to faith-infused determination in the face of personal adversity, Dr. Asp takes you on a courageous journey of perseverance, inspiration and hope. His honesty and bravery have proven to me that resilience is at our core, and that difficulties are not barriers, rather a chance to learn and adjust. He has convinced me that believing in yourself, setting far reaching goals and surrounding one's self with a supportive team will carry us along a path in life that is worth living!
Ben Popp
Executive Director
American Birkebeiner Ski Foundation

This engaging memoir is by a psychologist who at the age of forty developed into a serious athlete living the vacillations of mood that comes with high level competition. The descriptions of the mental and physical preparation and endurance required to do three Ironmans, a swim from Alcatraz to San Francisco, a Grand Canyon Rim to Rim run are more than enough rich material for this book. However, there is more. Years into competition the author is diagnosed with Stage IV melanoma. In alternating chapters Asp weaves these different kinds of challenges together and like two streams that eventually converge considers the question: What might be learned from high level competitive sports training when facing a challenge that doesn't confront you so much as strike at the back of your knees? Asp doesn't offer a trite answer to this question; instead the vivid descriptions let the reader have the experience of running in his shoes and considering how we might personally respond. I really enjoyed this book, and while it would appeal to readers of Outside Magazine, it would also be of interest to those grappling with serious illness. This book drives home the idea that while no one else can run the race for you, they do run it with you and if you are paying attention you can see the magnificent improbability of just how we inspire each other day to day.
Karen Schaepe Ph.D.

Inspirational! How Dr. Asp faces major challenges (some chosen, like the Ironman; some not chosen, like cancer) with perseverance and levity; his honesty about his fears and how faith, family and friends help to sustain him through his adventures.
Nancy Olson RDN, C.D.E.

Paralleling two battles, <u>Start Line and Beyond</u> is a deeply personal story of human triumph in the face of adversity. Alternating narration between his fight against cancer and for his physical and mental health through athletics, Dr. Asp outlines the people, places and moments that impacted his wellbeing. From triathlons to

marathons, and even an Ironman, Dr. Asp depicts the challenges and triumphs of combating our greatest fears. An inspiring testament to the human spirit, and a reminder to the reader to appreciate every moment we have, <u>Start Line and Beyond</u> leaves you with a feeling of gratitude and a motivation to live for today.
Megan Farmer M.A.
Chief-Social Media, J.P. Morgan
Vice President, Communications- J.P. Morgan Company
New York

This book is a remarkably honest, open and authentic account of the many challenges people face when going through cancer and the intense determination it takes to pursue and succeed in the often solo aspects of triathlon training. This is a must read for any racer, race fan or person seeking to understand how to push through the trials to achieve their goals. The stories of race comradery, highs and debilitating lows will make you want to sign up for the next marathon in your city. It's infectious! And the deep bonds and partnership between Dr. Asp and his fellow riders and runners is so inspiring.
Stephanie Goetz
Owner/CEO of Goetz Communications

David Asp is a person of faith, a psychologist, an athlete, and a cancer survivor. He mines each of these areas for wisdom which coalesce in this inspiring memoir. Readers beware—this book will have you attacking your own challenges well before the final page is finished.
Justin Boeding
Senior Pastor
United Lutheran Church-Red Wing

In <u>Start Line and Beyond, Chronicles of an Athelete/Cancer Patient</u>, Coach Asp candidly lays out the intimacies of his journey as an athlete and as a patient. The highs and lows, laughs and challenges that he has experienced serve as an inspiration for the reader. Written with humility, humor and honesty, Chronicles shares with us a worldview that can be used to face any challenge, whether it is chosen or unavoidable. Coach Asp's story is one of faith, determination and strength.

Emily Nagel
University of Minnesota Student
Former Member of Red Wing Nordic Ski Team

I am not one to sit still long and read a book, yet David's story writing captured me and I read <u>Start Line and Beyond, Chronicles of an Athlete/Cancer Patient</u> cover to cover. I loved David's story. I was riveted by his accomplishments and struggles as an athlete and cancer witness. David has an amazing attitude towards every challenge he faces whether in the middle of a grueling 12-hour race or when hearing news his cancer has spread. His ability to never give up and to always push his limits is contagious and inspiring.

Caitlin Gregg
Olympic Cross Country Skier and World Championship Medalist

Start Line and Beyond

Chronicles of an Athlete/Cancer Patient

Dr. David R. Asp

www.9footvoice.com

9 Foot Voice - Minnesota

Cover Art by Patricia Beckmann

Cover design by Erin Nausin
www.theprimaverastudio.com

and by Chloe Mark
www.chloemariemark.myportfolio.com

ISBN: 978-0-9968432-6-3

Photo credits: With the following exceptions, photographs are
from the author's personal library and were either taken by the
author and his family or the author is unknown: The Bob Cook
Memorial Hill Climb Poster on page 29 is courtesy of DP James,
www.lightandsoundgroup.com, ©2001; the map of the Border
to Border triathlon on page 40 and the Grand Canyon Rim to
Rim on page 158 is courtesy of Margaret Warner, ©2017; and
the Birkie Start on page 69 is courtesy of the Tony Wise Museum
of the American Birkebeiner ©1985 American Birkebeiner Ski
Foundation.

To my nephew, Kirk.
Your strength and courage in the face of adversity has inspired me for more than thirty years.

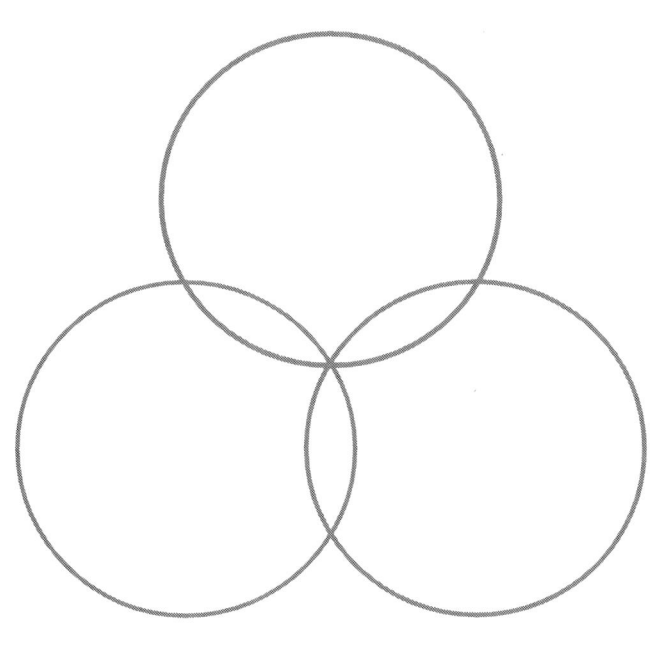

Table of Contents

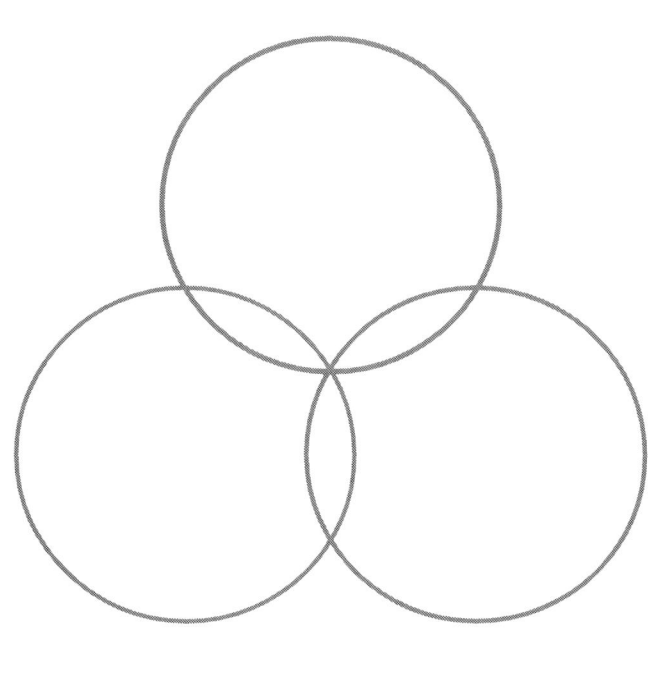

Forward

Dr. Asp's book documents his journey with cancer in the background of a lifetime of achievements, struggles, love, compassion and resiliency. Reading through the pages, I found myself cheering him on in an IRONMAN® race, worrying about the dangers of a possible war deployment, excited about a young married couple beginning their life together, distraught over his diagnosis of cancer, and encouraged by his resilience and faith.

As Dr. Asp so wonderfully describes in this story of his journey, cancer only occupies one small aspect in the mosaic of life. As devastating as this diagnosis can be, it is not greater than life and a person is never defined by it. It is simply an accident in nature that one has to deal with as best as one can. It does not have the power to control our lives.

- Svetomir Markovic M. D., Ph.D.

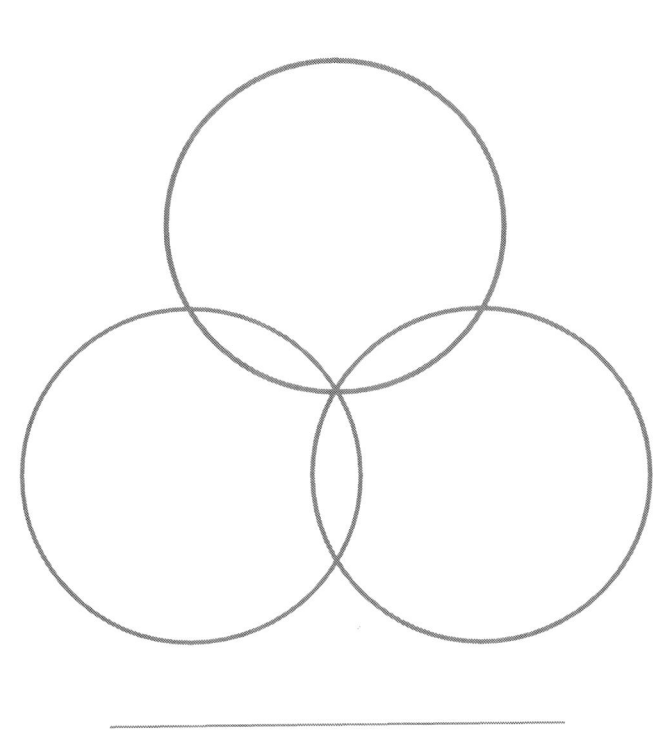

Acknowledgements

Writing a book is very much like training for an IRONMAN® event. It's taken enormous periods of time, consumed much of my thinking (thanks to my wife, Kathie, for understanding when I had that far off look in my eyes) and has often been the source of self-doubt. As with an IRONMAN®, it was tremendously helpful to have the encouragement from others. When friends would ask how the book was progressing, their positive and reassuring words were the impetus I needed to push forward through times of uncertainty. For all of you who asked, thanks for being there to make this dream a reality.

A special thank you to the members of Red Wing Nordic for their youth and energy. Your enthusiasm was contagious and helped bring me through the narrow parts of this adventure.

I want to especially thank Laura and Karl Rydholm for their insightful words and support both at our meetings at church and our home. To Kevin, my running buddy, thank you for accepting my grunts in response to your book inquiries while running. I wish I could have responded with more intelligible discussion but catching my breath was more important.

I am deeply indebted to the Mayo Clinic, particularly my medical team. The care they provided kept me alive. (I certainly couldn't have written this book had I been dead.) Mayo Clinic is a leader in cancer care and melanoma research. As a result of their expertise and care, I am allocating the majority of profits from this book to the Mayo Clinic Melanoma Research Center.

I would like to thank the Mayo Clinic Review Board, the Offices of Medical-Industry Relations and Conflict of Interest Review and the Mayo Foundation for Medical Research for their assistance and direction regarding business, confidential information, conflict of interest and medical relations.

I am tremendously grateful to have had the professional assistance of publisher, Brian Scott. We met many times during the course of this project. I appreciated his suggestions, ideas and the effort he put forward to make this dream of mine reality.

Many thanks to my sister, Patricia Beckmann, a retired art director who created the cover design for the book. Thanks to Chloe Mark for her assistance in graphic design. I deeply appreciate and thank Margaret Warner for her time and effort in designing the course maps for the Border to Border event and the Grand Canyon Rim to Rim run. Thanks also to Mike Clay, retired English teacher, for his permission to use his beautifully written poem of the American Birkebeiner. Thanks to my brother-in-law, John Farmer, for his review and thoughtful critique. And many thanks in so many ways to good friends Bob, Susan and Stephanie Goetz. Thank you for allowing me to interview you regarding two very personal and emotional tragedies.

To all the cancer patients I have met on this journey, thank you. Seeing your courage and hearing your stories provided me with strength, hope and inspiration. There is an old Chinese proverb: When the root is deep, there is no reason to fear the wind. Walking this uncertain journey together provided strength and seemed to calm the gales.

I am deeply grateful to my older brother, John, for his initial review and editing of this book. My brother captains a boat at Disney World and he says it like it is. Therefore, I knew he wouldn't mince words and would provide helpful criticism. He did, and for a while I thought I might be on the couch of a psychologist friend. My ego may have been bruised for a time but my brother's edits, thoughts and suggestions became the backbone of this writing.

Whether it's in the challenges of an IRONMAN® or cancer, people have tremendous stories of faith and resiliency. My brother and his family have their own remarkable resilient experience in coping with loss and suffering. Losing a daughter at age 16 from a congenital heart condition is a difficult loss in itself to bear for any family. Then in his mid-20's their only other child was diagnosed with a progressive atypical cerebellar ataxia. This progressive illness is

characterized by poor muscle coordination, tremor, problems walking, swallowing and speech. My brother, his family and his son Kirk, have demonstrated remarkable strength in coping with this progressive condition. Kirk, now in his early 50's, has been wheel chair bound for years. His pronounced tremor has slowly worsened making it difficult to talk and eat independently; and he experiences chronic back pain from a bulging disc. Still he continues, as much as possible, to ride his recumbent hand cycle bike, fish and live life as fully as possible. Because of his strength and courage in coping with his adversary, I dedicate this book to him.

Lastly, as they have throughout my cancer journey, Kathie, my two children Erik and Keri and their significant others have supported and encouraged me in this book project. I am indebted to my wife, Kathie, for her support, patience and unconditional encouragement. When doubts about this project were at its highest, she was always there with reasonable and positive words. After 43 years of marriage, my love for you has only become stronger.

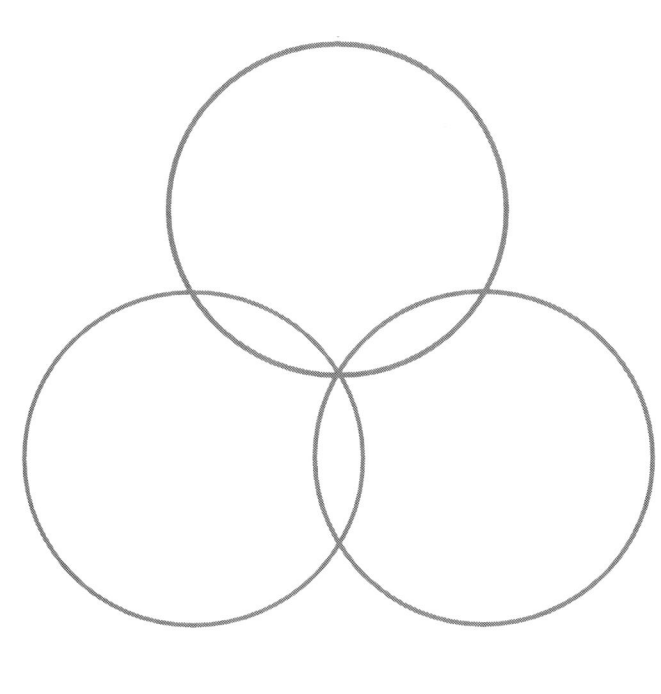

Author's Note

The events described in this book are based on my memory - even though that memory has faded as I've aged. Fortunately, I have been able to rely on detailed workout and competition logs that I kept for the IRONMAN® training and the fine memory of my dear wife, Kathie, who's been an integral part of virtually all my adult life.

In most cases the names of family and friends are real. I made an effort to obtain permission to include them in this manuscript. They have each played a significant role in my life and my adventures. I am deeply appreciative for the tremendous support and inspiration they bestowed on me.

The names of Mayo Clinic physicians and providers have either been changed or not included to protect privacy. I am immensely grateful, however, for the unparalleled care I received as a patient.

Equally so, the names of medications and treatment drugs are not included. For clarity and consistency, I have identified a medication by a letter of the alphabet.

The names and any identifying data of clients of mine, I have changed in order to respect confidentiality. Any resemblance to persons resultant of changing names or identifying details is entirely coincidental and unintentional.

Lastly, the views stated in this manuscript are entirely mine and should not be attributed to any other individuals, clinics or institutions.

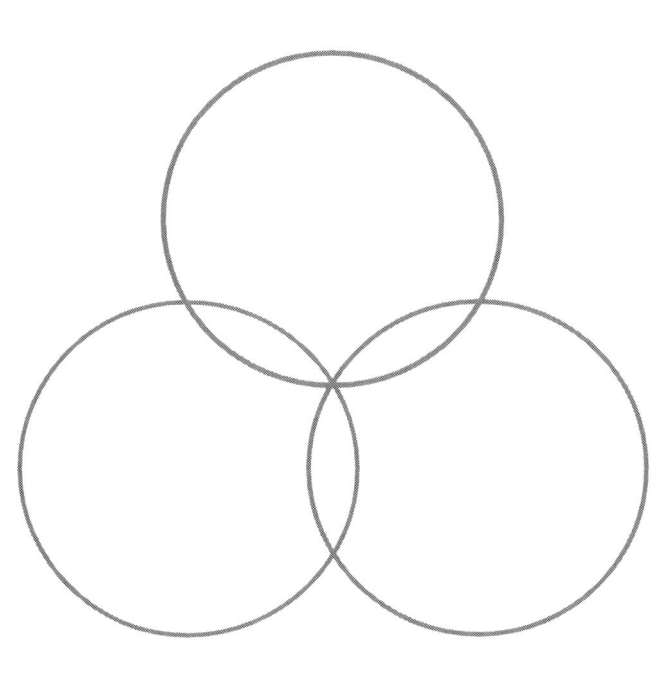

Introduction

I had one more mile to go before making it home. Soon the road would rise significantly up the hill, flatten on top, and follow a short, easy distance to the driveway. I had run the hill many times before, usually the last challenge of a workout, and frankly, I never looked forward to the arduous effort needed to get to the top. Since my legs were already spent, this time wasn't going to be any different.

It was early March 2015 and the weather was surprisingly comfortable for Minnesota, where winter rarely releases its grip so soon. I was zoned in on music when my phone rang. It took a moment as I struggled to catch my breath to realize it was my dermatologist. He was a runner himself with a positive, can-do energy, but that day his voice sounded grave. In a few short, carefully worded sentences, he said that the results of the PET Scan revealed my melanoma cancer had metastasized to the liver, bone and spleen. His words came in slow motion and brought my run to a stop. Listening to this news my immediate thought was, "Don't say pancreas." He didn't, but I was still stunned. I began sorting through the thoughts flooding my mind. In one phone call, the hill looming ahead suddenly became a monumental climb.

Life is a series of challenges, and my life, I suppose, hasn't been much different than that of most people. I had been in excellent health and medical challenges have been few. The diagnosis of cancer a year earlier, at age 66, didn't come as a great surprise as we have a robust history of it in my family. Now, however, with my cancer metastasizing to Stage Four, I found myself facing a serious life adversity resulting in an increasing awareness of my mortal existence.

Still I needed to climb that hill. I needed to finish my run and make it home. Moving forward despite the setbacks and failures is, I believe, an act of faith - and something we can only do with help and inspiration from God, family, friends, and kind strangers along the way. Identical elements that would be required, I trusted, for this uncharted new adventure.

This book is about faith and resiliency. It is estimated that, in a given year, 20% of people in North America will experience a traumatic event such as illness, natural disasters, personal victimizing experiences or major losses. How people cope with these challenges is mixed. While no one walks away from a traumatic event without experiencing considerable stress, most people show remarkable resilience (Meichenbaum 2012).

Research in resilience reveals that people who've had a history of moderate challenges in their life generally have lower levels of distress, less functional impairment, higher life satisfaction and well-being than did those individuals with no history of adversity (Meichenbaum 2012). The implication, of course, is that exposure to stressful life events can have a strengthening effect and help people handle challenging situations in the future.

For some, however, trauma and the stress it brings can destroy lives. It leads to worry, poor sleep, depression and a host of other medical problems. We can get bogged down in the grief of a loss or the injustice of a violation which tears a family apart and can separate us from friends or our spiritual faith. For instance, a diagnosis of cancer can lead a person to feel abandoned by God, angry at the world, and dissociated from their support.

Challenges, on the other hand, can be a catalyst to shake up old habits and enrich our emotional lives. Without life challenges we become complacent and too comfortable. We avoid pushing ourselves or taking risks. We follow the path of least resistance, avoiding the discomfort of physical activity or the uncertainty of unknown outcomes. Without challenges to test us, we quickly get frustrated and lose hope when small obstacles get in our way.

We need challenges but that doesn't make it easy to step out of our comfort zones. Carol Dweck in her landmark research regarding mindsets, has shown that the view one has of his/herself profoundly affects their ability to cope with life challenges. If we believe that our qualities - personality, moral character and intelligence - are fixed in stone, a need is created to prove ourselves. Every situation for people with a fixed mindset calls for a confirmation of their intelligence, personality or character. As a result, people with a fixed mindset are likely to shy away from challenges because those challenges are seen as threatening the view they have of themselves (Dweck 2006).

Dr. Dweck found another mindset where traits are continually being developed and realized; a mindset she referred to as a growth mindset. Although people may differ in their initial talents, interests, aptitudes or temperaments, everyone can change and grow through application and experience.

For those whose mindset is fixed, everything is about outcome. If they fail to confirm their image of who they are, then their self is seen as a failure. A growth mindset, however, permits people to value what they are doing regardless of the outcome. It is the process which is valued. Growth-minded people find the journey deeply meaningful. They have passion for stretching themselves and sticking to the course, especially if it isn't going well. This is a mindset that allows people to thrive during times of adversity (Dweck 2006).

While each of us has different levels of resiliency, we all can strengthen the level we have. Resilience does not come from some special or extraordinary quality. Rather it develops from using ordinary resources and everyday coping skills that we already have. Factors such as a positive attitude, flexible thinking, the degree of social supports and perceived personal control contributes to how well we adapt to adversities. In his resiliency training program (SMART) at Mayo Clinic, Amit Sood M.D. describes resilience thinking as anchoring our thoughts in timeless principles of gratitude, compassion, acceptance, meaning and forgiveness (Sood 2013). Lastly, for many, including myself, faith in a higher power plays a huge role in coping with the obstacles of life.

In the following chapters, I'm going to bring you along on the adventures I've had, and introduce you to the people I've met as I became a three-time IRONMAN® competitor and now a full-time cancer patient. This is not a "how to" book or an instruction manual. It's a book of stories and experiences I've had, some of them chosen and some bestowed on me. Some of these were epic highs and others frightening lows. In this book, I've chosen to loosely organize my writing by alternating chapters of my journey chronologically as a cancer patient with chapters describing many of my athletic experiences leading up to and beyond the 2008 IRONMAN® World Championship.

In each of the adventures there was an element of facing the unknown and the risk of failure, injury or even death. Each necessitated flexibility in plans because conditions would change or obstacles would get in the way. It was equally important to choose a positive perspective as much as possible even when it was most difficult to do. Each adventure had the support of others. No one else can run the race for you, but they can run it with you, inspiring and supporting you to move forward.

These are experiences that I, a cancer patient, now draw upon for strength and resiliency. Both the athletic and cancer journeys are filled with stories of adventures. They are filled with emotions, people, and faith which inspired me to dream, see possibilities and continue to confront the uncertainties of an unknown future.

As you will see, my family has shared these journeys with me. Through the years of events and training they have sacrificed their time and allowed me to spend countless hours away from home. They have been on the sidelines, usually cheering but sometimes questioning my crazy ambitions with mixed emotions. Being an athlete with a consumed focus can be a self-centered way of life and my family has graciously put up with events during vacations, my pre-race tensions and incessant talk of the event post-race.

Now with my cancer diagnosis, my family's lives have been significantly affected. It's their journey too, and they feel the effects of its highs and lows. They have had to experience the worries of an upcoming PET Scan, MRI or the uncertainties of treatment. I receive calls and texts from my children, Erik and Keri, asking how a procedure went and how I was feeling. Kathie has experienced sleepless nights and shared my fears and yet has been there every step of the way. As a Nurse Practitioner, she has been in consultations to ask questions, interpret results and hold my hand through the worst of it. Words simply cannot convey how important they have been and continue to be for me.

I have also experienced the presence of God on this journey. I don't know what God's plan is for me, but I do believe His sovereignty will bring out the good in everything. Already, cancer has drawn me closer to Him and my family, and, as a result, the burdens of this journey are eased. I believe any adventure, even one of suffering, increases our understanding and broadens our view of God's promise, encouraging us to be more compassionate and nourishing towards others.

My hope is that my stories will inspire you to follow your dreams and deepen your faith. I hope you will explore new possibilities and find the strength to unlock the chains which keep you from confronting your challenges. And if you are struggling with a chronic disease, I hope I can add to your resilience, your courage, your coping abilities and your faith so that every day is filled with dignity and purpose. We should not allow fear or anger of the C word - or any physical or mental problem - determine how we live our lives. We didn't choose to be a victim of our disease, but we have a choice in how we cope with our disease.

All IRONMAN® athletes begin with a dream, which then has to be translated into an enormous amount of hard work and determination. They must make a plan, then take it one step at a time. They push themselves, experience setbacks, discover limitations and, in the end, persevere to accomplish their goal.

I've discovered facing stage four cancer is a remarkably similar experience. In order to cope and to thrive, I needed to dream, to plan, to adjust to setbacks, and to take it one step at a time in order to persevere. Ultimately, the challenges that prepared me to be an IRONMAN® are now carrying me through the most difficult challenge of my life. I didn't choose to get cancer, but rather than a path filled with fear and bitterness, I've done my best to choose a path filled with hope, support and grace.

In the end, it doesn't really matter how well we do something, or if we win, or even if we finish at all. What matters is having the courage - despite mistakes and setbacks - to get ourselves to the start line again and again.

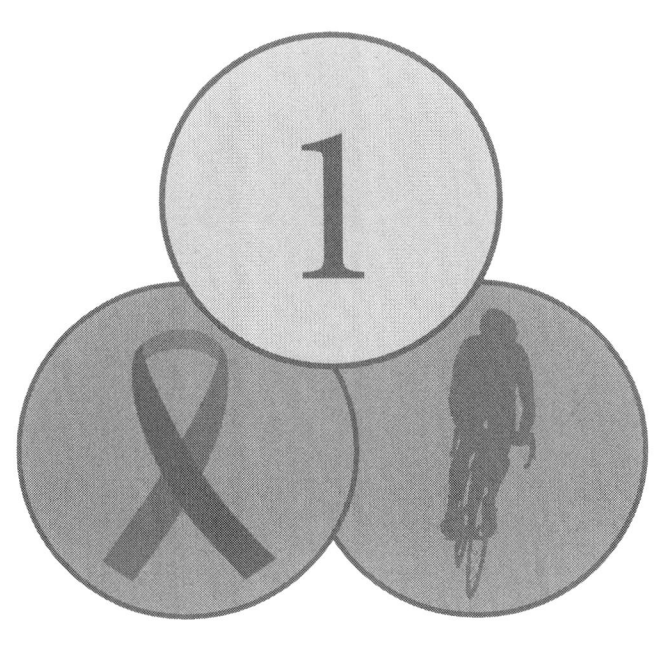

Basic Training

I wasn't a particularly brave or resilient kid and grew up in a pretty normal family. I came to find out in my work as a psychologist that all families have some dysfunction; it is just a matter of degree. And most children, even those who grew up in screwed up family systems, thought theirs was normal.

It was early morning and a humid haze had already surrounded the city. It would be another hot July day. I felt a slight pull in the backseat as Dad's big MerCruiser rounded a corner. There I was, a 24-year-old man who two days before had graduated with a Master's Degree. Now I silently longed for my mother to hold me and make this nightmare go away.

Dad made one last turn on the downtown street in Minneapolis where the Federal Building was located and where my induction into the U.S. Army would occur. Before me was a traffic scape full of people going about usual activities of their lives, getting to appointments, reporting to work. In a few seconds, my usual activities would no longer be usual. My life would take a dramatic and frightful change. I faced a challenge, a foreign world I didn't ask to be part of and one I was not convinced I could handle.

We reached our destination just as the stoplight had changed to red. There was no place to park so Dad pulled the car to the curb. Just a few seconds left before the light turned green. Just seconds left to say a few words.

There was too much to say. My parents had given me a good childhood with wonderful experiences. I was the youngest of three children. I grew up sheltered and spoiled. My father was a social worker. He had a strong work ethic and was the disciplinarian. My mother was a kind, loving woman who worked hard raising all of us while working full-time as a secretary. We were regular church-goers and I was taught important values of honesty, family and caring for others.

At age 12 before interstate highways and cell phones, my parents brought me and my siblings on our first great adventure. They piled us into our 1955 Oldsmobile loaded with maps, food and camping gear and took us on a three week road trip to California. It seemed like we saw every national park, attraction and did everything there was to do in the west including visits to the Badlands, Wall Drug, Route 66, Reptile Gardens, Rocky Mountain National Park, Hollywood, San Francisco and the old Giant Stadium where I saw Willie Mays strike out on three straight swings. It was a time of adventure and discovery.

But that had happened a long time ago. Now it was all changing. I watched with dismay as the light turned green. Wishing I had eternity not seconds, I said my goodbyes. I opened the door -leaving much unsaid - and turned toward the Federal Building.

It was 1971 and the war in Vietnam had not gone away. The government had recently introduced its lottery system, and I had drawn 151, low enough to receive my U.S. Army letter from President Richard M. Nixon. There was no way out and I was scared.

I took a deep breath as I entered the gray sterile confines of the Federal Building. Signs and paper footprints taped on the floor directed me to the new recruit section. It wasn't long before I was standing in my first line. I could feel my heart pumping. As we waited, several of us recruits began talking and we speculated that we would all be sent to the same military base. Our bodies were probed, papers were signed and after a long delay, my fellow enlistees and I were driven to the airport. We were flown to St. Louis and from there bussed onward to Fort Leonard Wood some 150 miles southwest. I was the oldest of the five to six of us on our way to Basic Training and with my newly awarded degree, probably the most educated.

As a child, I would never have imagined spending enough time in school to earn a Master's Degree. I spent my youth mostly developing a determination to avoid challenges and fear rejection. In my earliest grades, I had an embarrassing speech impediment which made it difficult to correctly pronounce the letters R and L. Additionally, I wore glasses and had braces to straighten my front teeth. I remembered being particularly mortified one day after receiving a new brace for my teeth that was bright pink and trying to hide from my classmates. My teacher saw it and thinking I had gum in my mouth told me to spit it out. With a red face, I stood in front of the class for an eternity trying to convince my teacher that the pink object in my mouth was a brace and not gum.

It doesn't take much of a childhood trauma to affect a person the rest of his life. One afternoon, a friend invited me to explore a little playhouse in his front yard. Unfortunately, when in the playhouse, he thought it would be funny to lock the door. Those few minutes in a tight, enclosed place I couldn't escape were a panic-stricken nightmare. The experience marked the onset of claustrophobia which would continue to haunt me.

For a while things grew worse instead of better. During grade school, I began to experience a sense of anxiety when it came to leaving home. Things like going to school, staying over at a friend's house or going to summer camp produced far more fear than excitement. This caused my self-esteem to take a hit.

By middle school I'd successfully become a mediocre student not excelling at any subject. I'd learned at home how to avoid work and responsibility and successfully transported these patterns of behavior to school. Teacher conferences were attempts to motivate me to buckle down and get serious. And the older I became, the more my parents became concerned about my future.

Then came 8th grade and Mr. John J. Anthony, a middle aged man of Italian descent. He had a full head of black hair, a stocky build and a large nose. He was my first male teacher and the first teacher who seemed to believe in me. He wasn't interested in only evaluating students, rather he wanted to encourage us. Subjects were taught with zest and consequently became more interesting. Mr. Anthony encouraged us to take risks. Failure or not knowing something was just another part of learning. And for that year I remember catching on, actually becoming excited about school, even excelling. Midway through the year, I actually stood up in front of the class and gave a speech. For the first time, I enjoyed it without feeling overly anxious.

It was a great year. Unfortunately, moving into ninth grade my enthusiasm didn't last and I fell back into the habit of doing as little as possible to get by.

I continued to scrap through to my senior year when I finally realized my lackluster school performance would be a problem. I had worked summer jobs as a dishwasher, steel supply worker and mosquito control laborer; it had convinced me that I didn't want to be doing those things all my life. My high school counselor, however, informed me that by his assessment, I wouldn't make it as a college student and he was confident that no colleges would even accept my application. My options were limited but as I didn't want to work, and certainly didn't want to be a soldier, I decided to go against my counselor's advice. Hoping for a miracle, I decided to apply to Mankato State College.

A miracle! Contrary to the counselor's assessment, Mankato accepted me. I continued to be a mediocre student and spent four years focused primarily on having a good time and studying just enough to keep a C/B grade level. In my sophomore year, I joined a social fraternity and by my senior year I was elected as social chairman. Under my authority we organized events which involved hiring local bands and obtaining a sufficient number of beer kegs for the participants.

Obviously lacking academic discipline, I became increasingly concerned about the growing war in Vietnam. It was the 60's, when an anti-establishment culture fueled by the civil rights movement and Vietnam War protests exploded onto the scene. My hair grew long. I was marching in anti-war protests and listened to Bob

Dylan, Joan Baez and other folk musicians. As Dylan wrote, "The times, they are a changing" and I was changing with them. The 60's counter culture was a revolution in social norms and a search for individual freedom, and it was affecting my thinking. As the war in Vietnam continued to escalate, it became increasingly clear that if I wanted to avoid the horrors of this confusing conflict, I had best stay in school to maintain my 2F status and avoid the draft.

I graduated with a relatively impractical undergraduate degree in psychology. Eager to maintain my student deferment, I enrolled at the University of Minnesota as a "special student," a category allowing me to stay out of the war and figure out where my life was headed. Fortunately, something began to stir within me while at the University. Perhaps it was the course work, or being at the "big" university - or perhaps, after all these years, I finally began to mature - but I found myself wanting to learn. Like eighth grade all over again, I started looking at my possibilities and potentials rather than my limits and constraints. I became more disciplined about reading and studying. Energized, I returned to Mankato State.

They had accepted me into their Master's Counseling Program on probationary status. On the very first day, my stoic graduate advisor told me that he and his colleagues would assess more than my academic work. They'd judge my character as well. So, with "probation" seemingly stamped on my forehead and the Vietnam War raging, I moved into a one room apartment, closed myself off socially and put my heart and soul into proving myself.

The Neumann Center became my home away from home. There, I learned to study as much as seven to eight hours a day. I was growing. In the past, even small obstacles or resistance would stop my progress and creativity, but I began to push through. I learned to master something takes time and effort. I remember being amused that throughout the semester the Center's study area was empty and I could always find a chair and table. However, when mid-terms and finals were close at hand the place was jammed with students cramming for their exams. I worked hard and the effort paid off. After two semesters, I was taken off probation and gained the respect of my advisor. I began to believe in my ability to learn. I had faced the challenge and damn, it felt good! A career in psychology became an exciting possibility.

But none of that would help me now that I was being drafted into the army. All the books I read, the tests I took, meant nothing. I was filled with uncertainty and fear. The only thing that mattered on that military bus was making friends and bonding with others. Strangers just a few hours ago, we knew we're going to need each other.

We pulled into Ft. Leonard Wood at two in the morning. The PFC's greeted us by screaming orders to get off the bus. A paranoid thought: Did they take me to a prison yard by mistake? Either way I was trapped.

Two PFC's directed us to a wooden WWII era barrack on post and ordered us to stand in line in front of bunk beds. In a harsh, demanding tone, they informed us we were now the property of the U.S. government. Exhausted and confused, I attempted to keep my mind focused to suppress feelings of panic. Again and again I pushed down the deep sense of uncertainty and tried not to worry if I would be able to mentally cope.

They called our first week in the Army "the Reception Center." During this time, they gave us haircuts, vaccinations, and uniforms, but my new buddies and I spent long periods doing nothing but worry and wait. This - when there was nothing to do - was the hardest part and the time I felt the most alone. By the end of the week, our Minnesota contingent had become acquainted with each other and familiar with the new routines. We were relieved that we'd all be going to basic training together.

On the last day of Reception Center we brought our duffel bags outside to an open area for a last interview, after which they'd ship us to basic training some three miles down the road. I stepped out with the others but fate took a hand. The sergeant, hearing that I had an advanced degree, kept me for a longer interview. I didn't think much of it, but when I returned to the open area, I found all the duffel bags, except mine, were gone. I stared in shock, feeling abandoned and tremendously alone. A couple of soldiers in charge decided since I missed my group, I needed to stay another day and go to basic training with the next group of enlistees tomorrow.

This was a nightmare. I pled my case, but the unsympathetic soldiers barely listened. My growing anxiety threatened to turn into panic. I had been left behind; I had lost my friends. I was alone in a strange land all due to a useless interview. But there was nothing to do but wait. As the hours passed, I prayed to God for strength. I reminded myself He was with me on this terrifying journey. The next day, after a sleepless night in an empty barrack, I found myself in a cattle trailer of a semi-truck on my way to basic training. The other recruits around me were complete strangers, mostly from the south.

It took years to realize how valuable this experience would be in my life. From the trials of being dislocated in the military emerged an awareness that I could survive even the darkest hell. I had prayed multiple times asking God to spare me from going and to take away my fears. He didn't. He had a different plan. Instead He stood by me and helped me face my fears. It took time but I emerged from the darkness understanding that if I could survive that, I could survive anything. This experience, as terrifying as it was, planted seeds which eventually sprouted in new confidence. It gave me strength to face the physical and mental challenges that came later in life.

From adversity comes advantage. I completed my basic training at Ft. Leonard Wood and was assigned to the medical division as an Alcohol and Drug Specialist. I spent two years on base counseling enlistees with substance abuse issues and veterans medically evacuated from Vietnam addicted to heroin and other drugs. I made many friends and, best of all, in the last year of my enlistment I met an Army nurse captain who was way out of my league. Her name, she said, was Kathie, and she would eventually become my wife.

Start Line

I was inactive, overstressed and overtired. I experienced frequent headaches and sleepless nights. I was 40 years old and needed a challenge, something to compel me off the couch. The final straw happened one morning when my wife called me plump.

Plump?! She called me plump! Shocked, I stood in front of the bedroom mirror and had to admit it was true. I was becoming rounder and developing mid-age belly rolls. I had to do something! A few days later I called my friend, David Roseen, and we decided to play racquetball at the local YMCA. I started slowly, twice a week for an hour each time. Our mantra was that nothing short of "life or death" would get in the way of our racquetball hour. Soon, I became the proud owner of a stationary bike and found myself sweating in my basement listening to 50's rock and roll music.

Still, I knew nothing about bikes or bicycle racing. It was the farthest thing from my mind. In fact, I suspect at that time, most of America knew little or cared much about even the biggest bike race in the world, the Tour de France. I didn't know there were amateur races as a part of summer festivals in many small towns around the region. I didn't know there was an association of more professional racers in the United States Cycling Federation (USCF) who staged races around the country.

One day however, my racquetball partner asked if I wanted to be a part of a relay triathlon. Twenty years later, triathlons would enter popular culture, but at the time, Roseen had to explain it was a relay event combining three events, swimming, cycling and running. Roseen, a marathon runner, would do the run and, knowing I'd sink like stone in water, he invited me to do the bike.

It seemed like an impossible idea, especially after hearing that I'd have to bike 56 miles, much of it over hills, when I couldn't imagine biking six! Still, I was trying to make a change in my life and had a couple of months to prepare, so I took the plunge and purchased a new steel frame Schwinn touring bike and began to cycle.

I started strong, but as time went on my internal critic increased in volume. That negative thought process inside my head put me down, doubted my ability and mocked my training. "You will come in last," it told me. "Who are you to think you should be in a triathlon race? You're not a real athlete. People will laugh at you." I did what I could to turn the volume down on these negative thoughts. I knew my thinking was unreasonable and told myself it was normal to have doubts.

Because of these doubts, I decided to enter a bike race to gain experience, build my strength and hopefully learn some strategies. Unfortunately, the race I picked, the Firehouse 50, was completely different than the bike segment of a triathlon. A triathlon bike segment is a time trial where drafting (biking close behind the biker in front of you to save energy) is not allowed; you're on your own racing against the clock. The Firehouse 50 is dominated by group riding and drafting behind a rider is not only allowed, but expected. Riders are also expected to take turns in front where there is more wind resistance. As the race unfolds, the faster, stronger riders break away from the slower riders so various packs form. Within each pack riders initially work together to maintain speed, stay in the lead or overtake the rider or group ahead. In the last few miles, however, it's everyone for themselves. It's all about who has the strongest legs and the right strategy for the final sprint.

The Firehouse 50 held in NW Wisconsin is one of the largest and oldest citizen's bike race in the United States. There were over 600 racers lined up shoulder to shoulder on the county road heading out of town; it was an intimating sight for a novice. I rolled my bike into the back sections of the start group and to my surprise, found myself next to Erik Gram, a physical therapist from my home town.

Gram was an amputee and sported a prosthesis on his right leg. In the years to come, he would become an inspiration to me. We would ride many miles together including one memorable ride mostly in a cold rain from Eastern Washington State through Idaho into Montana and Glacier National Park.

At the Firehouse 50, the minutes ticked down to the start and another rider heard this was my inaugural race. He briefly instructed me on the importance of drafting. "Stay within a foot or two of the rider in front of you, but don't touch wheels, because you'll go down." With the last warning in my head the gun went off and in the next few hours I became captivated by the thrill and excitement of bicycle racing.

After the Firehouse 50 I continued to train for the triathlon. My confidence was up. My internal critic was quieted. I thought I was ready for the race until the day before when my wife put her hand on my arm. "Be careful out there tomorrow," she said.

"What do you mean?"

"Well," she said. She looked worried. "I just want you to be safe. You'll be going up against real athletes."

It didn't do much for my confidence but still I was ready. The 56 mile bike portion of the triathlon turned out to be challenging with a significant number of hills to overcome. As a team, we completed it with a great sense of accomplishment. The experience also solidified my emerging passion for bicycle racing. And for the next few years, I became consumed with riding and attempted each summer to participate in as many races as I could.

The Cancer 5k

I t was late, the minutes had turned into hours but I continued to toss and turn. My head had been spinning and finally I mustered enough courage to speak.

"Kath, are you awake?"

She muttered something close enough to yes.

"Can I tell you something?"

In a soft voice she said, "Sure," and slowly turned toward me.

For a moment, I had a hard time finding the words, but finally I said, "I'm scared."

It was the PET Scan. I had a series of appointments coming up within the week at the clinic; none of them would be pleasant, but the PET Scan scared the hell out of me. Like millions of Americans, I struggle with anxiety, specifically claustrophobia. Those of us living with anxiety, whether it's generalized, an obsessive type or a specific phobia, tend to cloak our fear in silence because we worry what others might think. It has been particularly difficult for me as a psychologist since I assumed other people believe I should have the answers to fix the problem. Psychological strategies do help, but I'm not any more immune to emotional issues than a physician is to illness.

I had been married for forty years, but had never shared these fears with my wife. I had kept them hidden, put away. But now, just one day before the scan, I couldn't control my anxiety. I kept picturing an enclosed tube where I couldn't move and could barely breathe. It kept me awake long into the night until I knew I needed to talk about it. The more we can break the silence and tell our stories, the more the stigma of mental and emotional illness can decrease.

As Kathie had for the length of our relationship, she listened. She supported and comforted me. She didn't make me feel embarrassed about my fears but offered gentle encouragement. She reminded me that everything would work out.

The next day we woke early and drove to Rochester, Minnesota. With Kathie by my side, I checked in at the Nuclear Medicine Desk R in the Charlton Building. The receptionist's friendly smile didn't comfort me. Neither did the 5 milligrams of sedative I took do anything to do reduce my tension. They gave me a beeper and some forms to fill out, then directed me to find a chair in an already crowded waiting room. From two hallways, technicians were appearing and disappearing and their patient-summoning beepers were constantly going off. Watching this dance, I began to worry about what kind of technician they would assign to me. I planned on informing the technician of my fears and his/her response would be immensely important. I studied their faces as they waited for their patients, searching for the next Florence Nightingale or Mother Teresa. Which one would be mine?

All of this worry came from finding a bump. Some time after my annual physical in January of 2014, and having completed my 15th marathon in Los Angeles, I became aware of something on the upper back of my head. Was it a pimple, a scab? I couldn't see it. It didn't hurt or bleed but neither did it go away. A week later, my barber noticed it and expressed concern, so that afternoon I alerted my wife. Kathie was very concerned and demanded I immediately schedule to have it examined. Within a day, my dermatologist was removing a nickel size biopsy from the bump.

Having left my extraction in the hands of pathologists, Kathie and I left for the running of a half marathon in Fargo. On a Friday in May 2014, we headed north on Highway I-35 from Northfield, Minnesota. Immediately out of town we ran into road construction resulting in stop-and-go traffic. I grumbled in frustration.

With the delay we'd likely get caught in the Twin Cities rush hour. On top of that, the weekend was the state fishing opener so fishermen with their boats in tow would fill the highways heading north to lake cabins. I said to Kathie, "We're screwed."

A few minutes later I received a call from the doctor's office. A nurse informed me that the biopsy had exposed malignant melanoma 3.38 mm in depth. She told me the clinic would be calling on Monday to set up my next appointments, but by that point I had a hard time paying attention. After she hung up, I stared at the red brake lights in front of me as the information slowly sank in. I had a malignant cancer in my body. Feeling out of control, I was stuck in traffic and unable to unhear what I just heard! Maybe I really was screwed?

Melanoma? What the hell is melanoma? A pot luck dish made with melons? ("We'll be there and I'll bring my melanoma salad!"). I knew nothing about skin cancer or ultraviolet dangers. I certainly didn't know how or why I got it. I couldn't make sense of what the nurse had said, except the words "malignant" and "cancer" kept rolling around in my brain as we crept forward. Kathie, of course, was just as thrown off as I was by the diagnosis. Like the snail-paced traffic, we slowly reviewed the little information we had. There were alternating periods of silence mixed with expressions of feelings and thoughts as we attempted to put the news into perspective and develop a plan.

By the time we reached Fargo, Kathie and I had decided that until we had more information and a definitive plan there was no reason to inform anyone except our kids. Although the thought of cancer was persistently on our minds, the weekend went well. Our daughter Keri drove separately to Fargo as she was also running the race. We had run together before but this time I was more appreciative that we could run together shoulder to shoulder, side by side. She is an excellent runner, even when she hasn't trained adequately enough as was the case that day.

The day after the race, we told her of the diagnosis. It's always difficult to tell loved ones of negative news so we made sure we were alone and she had sufficient time to ask questions and express feelings. For a few moments Keri was silent as she attempted to process the information. As a family, we were entering unchartered territory and a look of fear was evident on her face. Perhaps not only for Keri, but ourselves, we voiced the importance of not jumping to conclusions until we had more information. Then we called our son, Erik. Like Keri, he had many questions. We assured both of them that we would keep them informed as the answers came.

Two weeks later I was at the clinic facing the dreaded PET Scan. As I sat stewing in the waiting room anticipating that my beeper would soon go off, I tried to remember the devotion I had read earlier that morning. It came from a book given to me by my dear friend, Bob Goetz. He was the first of many messengers from God I'd receive throughout my cancer journey. In Fargo, we stayed with Bob and his wife Susan at the home of one of their friends. The morning after the race I came into the kitchen where Bob was reading a devotional book while having coffee. In his unassuming way, Bob shared his faith which had been a rock of support for him through the deepest of tragedies. He wasn't pushy but was open about the strength and encouragement it had given him. Bob read devotions each morning to keep his faith strong and had an extra book back in Red Wing and wondered if I'd want it. We hadn't told him anything about the cancer yet, so I sensed God was extending his hand to me. That evening, after making the six hour trip home, Bob brought over his extra devotional book. I'd been reading it ever since.

Finally, my beeper started vibrating and then beeping on the side table. My head snapped up and my eyes searched the doorway for my Mother Teresa. Standing in the way, however, was a stocky, slightly balding man who looked like he used to play linebacker for the Green Bay Packers. As I walked to the doorway, I kept scanning the hallway for another tech, but there was no one else. The man was my technician and his badge said his name was Jack. I was not encouraged but when he asked me how I was, I blurted out, "I'm scared, I have claustrophobia."

Jack nodded, his face calm. He asked me to further explain and listened to my concerns.

He then said, "You could look at the machine first, if that would help."

I nodded and Jack took time to give me a tour of sorts. Gently, he showed me the machine and carefully explained the procedure. In his calm, accepting way, Jack did a great job of lowering my anxiety. He told me I'd have a way to signal him during the procedure which dramatically reduced my fears. Given his assistance, knowing more about the procedure and having a sense of control, I proceeded with the exam feeling more confident. In the end, the scan went remarkably well.

I had been so preoccupied with my anxiety of the PET Scan I hadn't had the energy to process the fact I had cancer. But after the test was completed, the reality of my situation set in. The next 24 hours were tedious with worry as we waited for the results. Finally, Kathie and I met my dermatologist and his nurse in the exam room. It was immediately apparent that he was a physician with great sensitivity and compassion. He listened carefully as I told him I didn't want any life expectancy predictions or hear that melanoma was chronic or incurable regardless of what the test results said. As a psychologist, I understood the tremendous influence a doctor's (or nurse's or technician's) statements can have in patient thinking. And I knew patient thinking affected attitude which may even affect the course of the disease itself. Negative projections breed negative thinking. Negative thinking adds stress and stress could negatively affect my immune system. What I wanted was hope and positivity.

My dermatologist delivered on both. He walked us through the tests and answered our questions in a warm, understanding manner. He told us the cancer hadn't spread, which was great news. But my primary site lesion was relatively deep. This meant I would need surgery by an ENT specialist to clear the margins, check surrounding lymph nodes and remove them if necessary.

In the process of the consult, my dermatologist mentioned he had been training for the Grandma's Marathon in Duluth. This prompted, of course, a discussion of our mutual interest in training and running. I had been a runner for 26 years and ran my first marathon (Grandma's) in 1989. It's not that I particularly enjoy running (I can count on one hand the number of times I've experienced runner's high) but compared to cycling, or cross-country skiing, running is easy to do. There's no bike to worry about, no skis to wax. Pull on a pair of shorts, lace up your shoes and you're off.

As our consultation wound down, my doctor told Kathie and I of a benefit 5K/10K run for melanoma research taking place in Rochester later in the day. To his surprise, I told him we'd be there. Back to Red Wing we went to gather up our run gear, then we turned around and drove back to Rochester. In short order, we joined more than 1000 participants in the 9th Annual Stay Out of The Sun Run.

Just hours after I'd been struggling with uncertainty and fear, I was running with my dermatologist in a 10K run. The event brought clarity into a hazy time. It reinforced the importance of not retreating from a challenge but moving forward despite my fears.

Rocky
Mountain High

A Man To Match Our Mountains
A life well lived is never lost.
Such lasting love it gives,
That this man's life will not be gone
so long as one man lives.
- Mary Alice Munger

Ever since our family trip at age 12, the Rocky Mountains have captivated me. As an adult, I would return to the mountains time and time again to reconnect with their beauty and inspiration. On this adventure, I wanted to push my limits as a seasoned cyclist and test my strength against the power of the mountain.

A mountain is awe-inspiring but there is a fine line between awe and fear. Oxygen levels are lower and conditions change in a heartbeat; temperatures can plummet in minutes and sunny skies can give way to thunderstorms or blizzards. Racing up the mountain was an adventure of facing the unknown alone. Skills I later realized I would need in my life.

I was fascinated when I first heard of the Bob Cook Memorial Hill Climb. It was an annual event organized in 1962 where riders raced up the treacherous 14,264 foot summit of Mt. Evans in Colorado. The idea of racing up a mountain was intriguing and, by that time, I was ready. I had competed in numerous races, accumulated hundreds of miles on the bike each year, and believed I was up to the challenge.

Bob Cook dominated the Mt. Evans Hill climb in Colorado from 1975 through 1980 winning the race every time it was held. He set course records year after year, culminating in a time of 1:54:27 in 1978. Over the years, some of America's best known cyclists added their names to the list of challengers, names such as Olympic gold medalist, Alexi Grewal, Jacques Boyer, Ron Kiefel and Andy Hampsten. But no name shone more brightly then that of the man whom the race now memorializes, Bob Cook.

Cook's lanky frame and wire-framed glasses made him look more like a scientist than a bike racer, but he could drive up steep passes like a mountain goat. While other riders succumbed to thin air, fatigue and pain, Cook could push his wiry legs to their limits.

Cook also competed in other major races, such as the Coors International Bicycle Classic and the 1980 Olympic Trials. He had a distinguished career in cycling ahead of him until late in 1980 when he began to experience headaches and balance problems. CAT Scans and exploratory surgery confirmed the presence of tumors spawned by multiple metastatic melanoma. Cook heroically fought his illness for three months, but the cancer proved stronger than even the strongest hill climber. Bob Cook died in March 1981 at the age of only 23.

Long before I knew anything of melanoma, what had been Bob Cook's bike challenge on the mountain I wanted as my bike challenge. What I didn't know then was that years later, I would be on a journey of medical challenges similar to his.

In July I drove my rented car past North Platte, Nebraska anticipating my first look at the snow capped peaks of the Rocky Mountains. Along Interstate 80 heading west, the Platte River bottom gave way to the rolling cattle-grazing high plains of Colorado.

Crossing the border near Julesburg, I remembered seeing Colorado for the first time at age 12 in the back seat of a 1955 Oldsmobile. My family stopped to take a picture standing by the colorful welcome sign on our grand tour of the west going all the way to California. Now, some forty years later, I had returned again to the west, this time headed for the Indian Hot Springs hotel in Idaho Springs and the Handlebar and Grill where I would pick up my number for the 2001 edition of the Bob Cook Memorial Mt. Evans Hill Climb.

I entered the Handlebar, and walked through the main drinking area to a back room where race volunteers were registering participants, handing out numbers and giving information about the course. The start, at an altitude of 7,540 feet, would be at Clear Creek High School near Idaho Springs on Rt. 103. For 13 miles we'd follow a consistent, but not dramatic, uphill grade to the junction of Colorado Rt. 5 at Echo Lake. At 10,600 feet we would follow Rt. 5 past the lake and then begin a dramatic rise past the tree line 15 more miles to the summit, finishing at an altitude of 14,264 feet. The entire 28 mile course would have few downgrades and only a couple of level sections.

After explaining the route, they gave us safety alerts:

A. Sudden weather changes are common on the alpine tundra. Daytime temperatures often do not exceed 60 degrees and can plummet with the arrival of a cloud or the stirring of the wind.

Above tree line, snow can fall on any day of the year.

B. Dress warmly. Temperatures drop 3-5 degrees for every 1,000 feet of elevation gained.

C. If caught outside in a lightning storm, retreat to the relative safety below the tree line or find refuge in a vehicle.

D. Exposure to the sun is 40% greater at this elevation than at sea level. Sunglasses and sunscreen with a rating of 15 or higher are recommended.

E. Above the tree line, there is only 40% of the oxygen available at sea level. Shortness of breath and fatigue are common effects.

Hearing about the course and reading the safety alerts, it began to dawn on me the significant challenge ahead. On a mountain, just as in life, changes can occur quickly. While

we usually cannot choose what or how things may change, we can choose how we adjust and respond. When change occurs, it will be important to alter my thinking to help see this variation in a positive way.

They also told me I could sign up for a van ride down the mountain when I finished, but I turned the offer down. If I put effort into climbing the mountain, I wanted at least to enjoy the relaxed ride down. This would turn out to be a big mistake!

I spent the night at the historic Indian Hot Springs Hotel, snuggly nestled in the mountains near Idaho Springs. The hotel sits alongside Soda Creek which years ago was the dividing line between the Ute and Arapahoe Indian nations. Both the Ute and Arapahoe Indians considered the natural hot springs sacred and the healing waters a place of the Great Spirit. For them, it was a place to worship and heal the sick. In 1863, Dr. E.M. Cummings built a log frame house near the hot springs and began charging visitors for health baths. Eventually this became the hotel. Records indicate that Frank and Jesse James, Billy the Kid, Walt Whitman and the Roosevelts have been among the many visitors. In more recent years, famous entertainers like Clint Eastwood, John Denver and Leon Russell have stayed at the resort.

I slept well and the next day awoke to fresh mountain air filled with the smell of aspen and pine. I hurried out of bed intent to acclimate myself to the elevation and loosen my legs with light cycling. By late morning I had dressed in cycling clothes, inflated my tires and began cycling east on Soda Creek Rd into the mountains. My ride started out beautifully through thick aspen and spruce forests and with frequent mountain vistas. The road climbed gradually and within a few minutes, my breathing grew labored. About an hour into the ride, however, conditions went south. The sun and the warm air disappeared. Quickly, the skies darkened, temperatures plummeted and the winds gusted - seemingly from all directions.

I grew alarmed and remembered the safety alerts we received at registration. Though I had been planning this for months, the dramatic change in weather from serene to ominous caused me to finally grasp the real risks of this undertaking. I decided it had been a long enough practice ride and turned around.

Back at the hotel I wondered what I had gotten myself into. The excitement I usually felt before a race had turned into something closer to fear. In less than 24 hours, I'd be riding the Mount Evans Hill climb in Colorado. Not only would the ride be physically demanding, treacherous weather could stop me from reaching the summit. I had come from the Minnesota plains and was questioning any business I had being in this race.

But I wouldn't let my fear stop me. I took a deep breath and reminded myself to adjust my thinking and see the next day's challenges in a more positive way. I had come all this way, I was a seasoned cyclist and this was going to be an adventure. No matter what, I certainly wasn't going to turn back.

The next day I lined up with 45 cyclists in the Senior Men's 45+ category group. I had raced enough to know that while the category was described as "senior men" the riders would be strong and experienced. The other option would have been the Citizen's category which was more suitable for novice riders. There were excellent riders in that group, but having come this far to race, I made the decision to test my abilities with the big boys.

We had sunny skies for our 9:00 a.m. start. The gun went off and we surged forward along Rt. 103. There was a yellow line rule which forbid riders to cross into the opposing lane so the pack of riders crowded along on the right side of the highway. It was all I could do to stay relaxed and find a place halfway near the front. My goal was to keep with the lead riders for as long as I could, even though I was a "flatlander" and suspected most of my competitors lived along the Rockies.

Soon, the pace began to quicken. Several riders could not keep up and got dropped off the back. As Rt. 103 continued its gradual incline, the group decreased in size and I felt more confident. Then, about 4 miles into the race, the lead pack of 25 decided to push the pace in an effort to eliminate weaker riders. I hung on during the surge but my legs and lungs began to burn.

Finally, the strongest leaders slowed the pace. The road continued up but I tried to stay relaxed and regain strength. I knew the break wouldn't last, but the next surge came sooner than I hoped, and my legs and lungs were on fire. Five more riders dropped back.

Silently I hoped we'd hit the end of the surges and could all go up the mountain together. But what the hell was I thinking? It was a race! Within minutes the leaders again increased the speed until it was too much. I began to drift off the back. I peddled faster and adjusted gears trying to catch up but the gap from the lead group expanded. It only took a matter of seconds, but I found myself facing the next 24 miles of steady incline all on my own. I slowed my pace to catch my breath and tried to ease into a relaxed rhythm.

Ten miles into the race I reached Echo Lake at 10,600 feet of elevation. At this point, the course took a right on Rt. 5 which we would follow all the way to the summit. After passing Echo Lake and its historic Log Cabin lodge, the road narrowed and became significantly steeper as it cut through spruce and aspen trees. Eventually, I passed Goliath Peak at 12,216 feet and the Mount Goliath Natural Area which has one of Colorado's few stands of bristlecone, which are some of the oldest trees on Earth.

At this stage, several riders who dropped earlier from the group caught up and passed me. I attempted to stay on a wheel but with the steeper inclines it was all I could do to keep peddling. After an initial feeling of discouragement, I was able to turn my thinking and strengthen my resolve to make it to the summit. On this day, I would simply refuse to let the mountain beat me.

I hit 13,000 feet and passed Rogers Peak. Before long I reached the tree line marking the change to rock and alpine tundra. At this elevation, the road no longer had guard rails so I became very conscious of not wandering too far to the right as drop offs were dramatic. After passing Mount Warren, I reached Summit Lake. Here the road actually took a short decline and I was able to briefly rest my legs.

From there, I climbed away from the lake. With five miles to go, it seemed as if the mountain would never end, but with steady turns of my small ring, I cranked closer to the top. The final few miles of the 14th highest mountain in Colorado became a snake-like segment of tight switchbacks. The road narrowed further and seemed to grow steeper at each turn. I stood on the pedals for the first time to make the grade. My legs burned with each crank. I had only a few more switchbacks to negotiate and seeing the finish ahead restored enough power to make it over those. Finally, I rolled over the last one and coasted my bike into the small parking lot atop the mountain.

A great sense of relief and peace as I soaked up the epic view. The blue sky vista at over 14,000 feet was spectacular. As I turned for 360 degrees I could see our beautiful earth go on forever. Encountering something so much larger than myself gave me perspective and I gave thanks to God for the moment. It took me 2 hours, 51 minutes and 24 seconds to climb the mountain, placing me 39 out of the 45 riders in my category. I wasn't able to stay with the lead pack, but I was thrilled to have experienced what Bob Cook experienced so many times in his short life.

On the other side of the parking lot, riders were climbing into vans for the trip down. As I watched them, it sank in that my decision to bike down was not, perhaps, the best one. I was drained of energy.

I had expected the ride down would be easier than riding up, but quickly realized nothing could be further from the truth. The descent was a frightening and exhausting journey. I needed to brake constantly as the gravity-weighted bike wanted to keep picking up speed. Careening on roads with no guard rails and drop offs into the abyss created more tension than any effort I exerted on the way up. And while I had not stopped once during the race, I needed to stop four times on the way down to get a grip on myself.

By the time I reached the high school parking lot I was wiped out. Still, I felt a great sense of accomplishment. On journeys to the mountaintop, no matter how long or short, the road will vary and often grow steeper. Fear and discouragement will shake our confidence. When this happens we need to stay the course and trust God will provide us with strength. I took a last look towards the peak. I had succeeded not only in conquering the mountain of Bob Cook, but conquering the challenge within myself.

I stowed my bike in the car, changed clothes and began the 15 hour drive home.

Border

to

Border

*"One of the longest and most challenging triathlons
in North America"*

*I don't know who on our team initially came up with the idea of
signing up for the Border to Border Triathlon. Decisions like this
are often made after a group has enjoyed a round or two of liba-
tions and I suspect this was the case with us.*

*The Border to Border triathlon was a race of cycling, running
and canoeing. All three of us felt comfortable as cyclists and runners, but none of us were confident in the canoe. It was a 50 mile
route on an unknown river in the far reaches of northern Minnesota. However, when the three of us made the decision, we made it
with the understanding it was a team effort and we were going to
do everything we could to be competitive.*

*Personally, I had turned 52 and knew most of our competitors
would be younger; I wanted to see if I could still compete. Could
I keep pace on the bike, run and canoe especially knowing two
teammates were depending on me? Also, on our team was a young
competitive physician who would drive hard in all three segments.
Could I still keep up with someone like him?*

*We all had our own individual objectives, but in the end we
were in it together, including our two friends who drove the team
van. This adventure required planning, communication, positive
attitude and a flexibility to change when faced with obstacles.*

T he Border to Border Triathlon, has been described as one of the longest and most challenging triathlons in North America. It was a team event of two, three or four person teams and began in southwestern Minnesota and wound its way to Crane Lake, a few miles from the Canadian Border. Over four days, my two teammates and I would cycle 400 miles, run 50 miles and canoe 50 miles to the finish.

My teammates on Team Red Wing were intense competitors. At age 52, I was flanked on one end by Rick Mollgaard, a 30 year old physician whose easy going style masked a fierce nature. I knew he would drive hard in all three segments. On the other end was Dave Roseen, a multi-marathoner who, at age 60, was in superb condition with no signs of slowing down. Together we had signed up with the intention of doing well and placing in our division.

Personally, I also wanted to find out if I was up to the challenge of going against my competitors, most of whom would be younger. Age has a way of sneaking up on us. Mysteriously, as years accumulated, just getting myself out of bed and onto the floor took a greater effort. Strange aches and pains seemed to come and go and injuries took longer to heal. But I wasn't ready to admit I was over the hill and felt I could compete with my teammates, especially knowing they were depending on me.

The canoe event was our team's soft underbelly. I was particularly concerned as I had little experience with it. I had heard expensive ultralight carbon paddles could improve efficiency and struggled whether to buy one. My wife, however, wasn't buying any of it and adamantly opposed my spending another penny on this race.

The We-No-Nah canoe factory in Winona, Minnesota was an hour and half south of Red Wing and had a small showroom of canoes and gear. Over my wife's objections, I drove to the factory to check out the paddles. An attractive clerk welcomed me into the store and directed me to their ultra light paddles. Naturally, anytime one evaluates a sophisticated piece of sporting gear in the presence of a knowledgeable (and good looking) saleswoman, it's important to demonstrate that you know what you're doing. So, I picked out one of the paddles and began a nice smooth paddling motion as if I were cruising down Crane Lake in first place with the finish line in sight. I slipped into a semi-conscious state as my imagination saw hundreds, no thousands of people at the water's edge cheering, waving, chanting…go…go…GO! Models in bikinis cheered alongside representatives from Nike waving contracts at me; it was a glorious finish!

"Sir?"

I looked up and realized the young woman was watching me with puzzled attention. With a slight hesitation she added, "You're holding it backwards."

"Oh," I said. And with that, I quickly turned the curved side around, bought the damn paddle and drove home wondering how I was going to explain this to my wife.

While my new paddle gave me some unearned confidence, I was still concerned about the canoe segment, so, a month before the event, Dave and I decided to participate in a canoe race on Lake Calhoun in Minneapolis. We hoped it would strengthen our prowess and build confidence. When we lined up with 25 other boats our expectations were running high knowing we had logged plenty of canoe training time. A few minutes before the start, a woman in a canoe next to us noticed our gear. "Look Steve," she said to her partner, "they have carbon paddles. They must be good." I gave a short look around and wondered why my wife wasn't here to hear that. Dave and I glanced at each other trying to maintain some humility, but inside our confidence was soaring.

From the mountaintop to the valley, it only took seconds before that confidence came crashing down. The gun went off, the other teams sprinted out into the lake but we were slow as molasses! The woman next to us and her partner soared ahead (with wood paddles) as Dave and I were treading water. Once underway, we desperately tried to catch up, pulling hard on our fancy carbon paddles, but to no avail. The other teams were faster and we finished dead last. We quietly paddled to the finish with our tail between our legs. We left the race venue quickly, praying we wouldn't see the woman who started next to us.

The experience rattled us and gave us a piece of humble pie. But setbacks are reasons for comebacks. Our poor showing gave us the opportunity to assess what went wrong and where we needed to improve technique and conditioning. Despite the failure, our attitude is what we make it; we needed to change our viewpoint to stay motivated.

Finally, it was the day before the race. After a five hour drive, our team arrived in Luverne, a small Minnesota community that sits in the southwestern corner of Minnesota. This is flat, lonely-looking farm country focused on growing corn, soy beans and sugar beets. The wind is a constant companion and brings in the various smells of rural life. Looking west beyond this little hamlet into South Dakota, the farmland continues until it gives way to rolling hills that climb in elevation all the way to the Rocky Mountains.

We stayed at the Cozy Inn, a mom and pop establishment straight out of the 1950s. Amenities at the single-story motel were limited to a telephone and single coke machine that sat outside the one room office. Crammed together and full of pasta, the four of us experienced our own farm odors as there was plenty of flatus expelled throughout the night.

The next morning, relieved to get some fresh air, I warmed up cycling the streets of Luverne. It was quiet with little traffic as I rode past farm implement dealers, grain and seed stores. It would be a good bet that few in town, if any, knew that Luverne was the

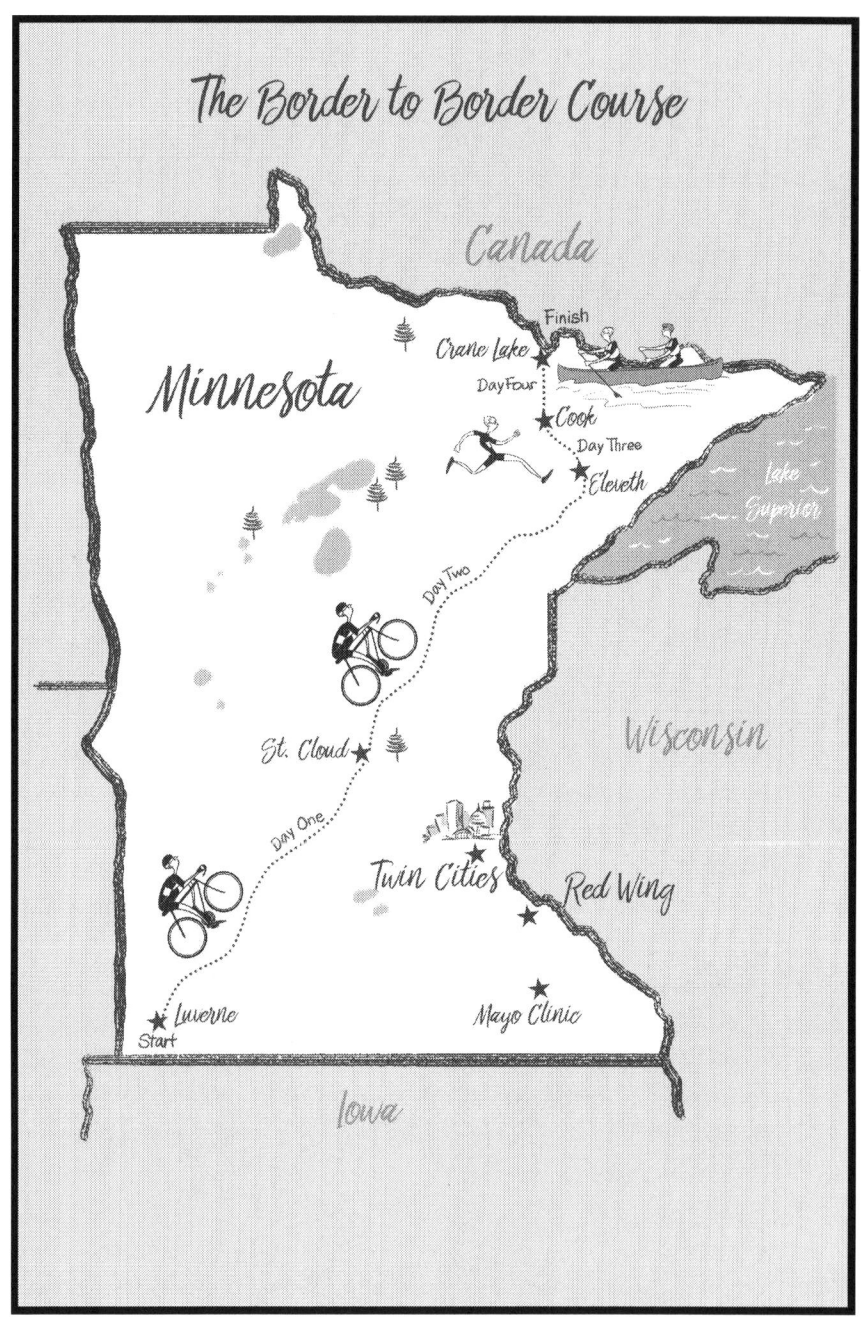

start of the 19th Annual Border to Border Triathlon.

This year there were a total of 35 teams registered, including the seven 3-person teams we would be competing directly against. Participants came from all over the United States including Maine, Tennessee, Wisconsin and North Dakota. Additionally, a team from Canada was entered. There were young, hard core athletes mixed with middle-aged competitors who seemed more relaxed. Some teams included female participants and there was one all-female team.

After completing my warm-up, Rick, Dave, Kevin and I gathered near the start line for a last minute briefing. In a few minutes, I would be cycling 12 miles then transition to Rick who would cycle to the town of Pipestone. There, Rick would transition to Dave. Kevin Bollum, Roseen's son-in-law, would drive the van and keep track of race details for the first two days of the race.

As time wound down to the start, a number of spectators gathered near the start line as cyclists moved into position. I pushed my bike, a Trek 5500 carbon frame outfitted with aero bars, near the front and clipped my right foot into the pedal. A cyclist in his late 20s with streaked blond hair pulled up alongside me. He was a member of the Canadian three-person team, the Boomtown Outfitters. He was sitting on a fully equipped triathlon bike with a rear disc wheel and I suspected he would set the pace. A wave of concern passed through me; this young cyclist would be the one to hang with, but I just wasn't sure I could.

I did what I could to dispel thoughts of self-doubt. I reminded myself that I was a seasoned cyclist. I had trained hard for this. And I had a great team supporting me.

The gun went off and cyclists surged forward to start the race. Sure enough, the blond Canadian sprinted into the lead on the highway heading north to Pipestone. I immediately jumped on his wheel and six of us started pulling away from the others by the time we hit the outskirts of town.

It didn't take long, a few miles, and my heart rate had skyrocketed and I started gasping for air. The young Canadian continued to pull, intent on remaining at the front. I continued to hold on, impressed at how strong he was as we hit speeds around 30 mph. It was an exhilarating experience but twelve miles later I was happy to approach the first transition point. Rick, the 30-year-old physician, had already cycled up to speed and he smoothly took my place. Relieved, I collapsed into the van as Kevin racked my bike onto our rear bumper carrier and drove us north to Pipestone.

In Pipestone, we saw Rick and two other cyclists who had opened a considerable lead from the rest of the field. Dave prepared his bike for the next leg. He was primarily a runner and would cycle shorter intervals to save his legs. Dave's transition went smoothly and he held his own on the highway so that Team Red Wing continued to pull away from the field.

Two other teams led with us: Team Sugoi, a two-person team who had won this race a number of times; and the three-person Canadian team, which included the blond cyclist. (Later, we learned that the Canadians and their wives had traveled 750 miles from Saskatchewan to compete in this race and, individually, they had participated on Canadian National Teams and triathlons all over the world.)

The course continued flat with occasional gradual inclines which did not allow any break in pedaling. With that, and a steady headwind beginning mid-morning, it made for a tough day. Thanks to exertion and increasing temperatures, we consumed a significant amount of water and Gatorade. When not driving, Kevin rotated our bikes to insure that the bike of the person on deck was in the van ready to quickly unload. Considering all the gear, clothes, food and accumulating garbage he had to work around, this was not an easy task.

As we approached the Mississippi River and the first day's destination the terrain changed to rolling green hills, broad valleys and thick forests. Finally, we pulled into St. Cloud having clocked a time of 8 hours and 41 minutes. Team Red Wing was in second place in the three-person division and third overall. The Canadians had beat us by 25 minutes and the next three-person team, Twisted Chicken, was 30 minutes behind us. We still had a long way to go, but were encouraged that we had done so well.

The next morning came quickly. After breakfast and pumping up tires I lined up for a mass cycling start. The gun went off and we followed a route which took us to the southeast shore of Mille Lacs Lake, a 22 mile long and 14 mile wide body of water named by early French explorers for "1000 lakes."

As we headed farther north the economic conditions of the area grew more depressed with fewer houses and more abandoned buildings surrounded by junk cars and debris. Some of the houses appeared to be guarded by what looked like 200 pound attack dogs waiting for some fool in brightly colored lycra tights to come riding by.

Turned out, I would be that fool.

About a quarter mile up the road, another team's car pulled into a driveway to transition their riders. Within seconds, two raging beasts the size of polar bears charged the car, hungry for fresh meat. In a split second, amidst a cloud of spattered gravel, the team car catapulted out of the driveway and down the road leaving those mongrels with only one target left: me, approaching in lycra tights, terrified to death and feeling bare-ass naked.

I stood on the pedals and pushed as hard as I could. My heart rate exploded as I veered wide planning for their attack but… the dogs stopped. They only looked at me as if they were granting passage into the farther, darker reaches of the remote north. I slowed down to catch my breath and wondered, What the hell am I doing here?

Throughout the day the wind had increased, becoming brutal by the time we arrived in Eleveth, our day's destination. Eveleth lies on the Mesabi Iron Range, once the richest source of high grade iron ore in the world. Reminders of past mining activity were scattered everywhere. Imposing open pit mines could be seen near thick stands of aspen which had reestablished themselves on the massive piles of ore tailings.

As we checked into the Eveleth Inn, Chuck Balzer arrived from Red Wing with our canoe. Chuck was replacing Kevin and would provide support our last two days. We all went to bed early as the next leg was a daunting 50 mile run to the little town of Cook. This would put us in position for the final section of the triathlon, the dreaded 50 mile canoe race to the finish in Crane Lake.

Early the next morning we dropped Dave off at the start line. He was our strongest runner and would take the longer segments of the course. The rest of us drove to the two mile transition point. There, I met one of the members of Twisted Chicken, the team challenging us for second place. He was young, friendly and psyched for the run since that was his team's forte. He told me his team had canoed the course on the Vermillion River to familiarize themselves with the route. Already nervous about the run, the conversation didn't help. My anxiety soared and I silently cursed myself for engaging him.

Soon, however, Dave came into sight and my mind could focus on the task at hand. By the two mile mark, the runners had spread out but Dave was near the head of the pack. We made the transition and I was off.

To be honest, running has hardly been an activity I looked forward to, and my legs felt heavy from the last two days of cycling. I'd run enough, however, to know that like many things in life, the first few miles are often the hardest. This is the time when people experience discomfort and doubt - and often quit. As hard as it is, I've learned to keep moving forward and continue the effort because in most cases, my condition (physical and mental) improves. And sure enough, as I pulled away from the outlying population of Eveleth, I settled in to a more comfortable run.

Initially things were going well but about a third into the race, it was clear that Dave's pace had slowed. The next time he was in the van, after gentle questioning, Dave admitted he had re-injured a hamstring. Over the next few stages, he gallantly tried to keep running but his injury grew progressively worse. At the 25 mile mark he was out.

We were only halfway and had lost time. Team Roadkill, whom we had been even with for much of the race, had pulled in front. The Twisted Chickens were far ahead. While disheartened, the setback wasn't going to stop us. We knew we had to restart and be flexible in our thinking. Having a plan is having hope so we were

On the run somewhere near Cook, MN

determined to structure a plan which would help us regain time. Rick and I decided that we could alternate running half mile segments to keep our pace up.

It helped. Seeing the van ahead and knowing that rest was coming soon lifted my spirits. It also helped that Chuck was recording the times for our individual sprints which created a sense of friendly competition between us. I was determined to keep pace with Rick. Despite little time for recovery, we maintained a consistent pace and began to close in on the other teams. Our confidence grew as Van Commander Chuck renamed the Twisted Chickens the "Toasted Chickens."

By mile 40 however, my legs felt dead so we decreased our segments to 3/10ths of a mile. Still, it was all I could do to complete those. Until we reached the finish in Cook, those brief minutes of rest in the van were heaven on earth.

Finally, it was over and Team Red Wing settled into a bed and breakfast nine miles outside of Cook on Lake Vermillion, where the canoe portion of the race would start the next day. It was a beautiful lake 40 miles long with 1200 miles of shoreline and 365 islands - or so I had been told. Honestly, I couldn't have cared less about the scenery. My goal was to find the nearest bed and rest.

After a two hour nap, I awoke to find Chuck, Dave and Rick discussing strategy for tomorrow's canoe event. The main concern was where to make our transitions since Dave's hamstring would hamper him from running the portages. After studying local topographical maps of the region, Chuck found Fire Road 601 which would bring the van to the river for the transition. The spot looked perfect. It split the course more evenly and gave Dave only one portage to negotiate. A call to a local resort revealed that the road was passable albeit "somewhat bumpy in places." That information confirmed our decision and it would be a go for tomorrow.

The morning's start would be at 5:30 a.m. with a required check in an hour before, so we headed to bed early. It was quiet in the B&B and most of the lights were out as I laid out clothes and equip-

Roseen, Mollgaard and Asp with racing canoe

ment for tomorrow's race. The canoe, of course, was outside, but my expensive racing paddle sat close to my bed. It didn't give me much comfort. The reality of canoeing 50 miles and running 11 portages in the wild reaches of the north woods was both exciting and frightening.

The next morning, with light of the sun barely tinting the sky, Rick and I paddled out to wait for the starting flare. The minutes passed and my anxiety crept skyward. We were fighting small waves to keep the boat pointed straight ahead and away from the others. The initial push would be hard. We had never seen the course or experienced a race like this. And damn, the canoe was tipsy. What if we swamped it at the start? My internal critic shifted to the Lake Calhoun disaster when we came in dead last, but I pushed the memory away. I took a breath and turned my mind to positive thoughts. We can only make our best effort, I told myself. Life doesn't depend on this canoe event. We have trained and handled this canoe before. As the seconds ticked down, I simply repeated in my head, We can do this.

It was deadly quiet when the flare rocketed into the predawn sky. We started off, but immediately found trouble when the boat heaved to one side. For a horrifying moment, the gunwale was less than an inch from the water. Waves from the other boats splashed over the edge. We both leaned hard against it, the canoe adjusted and we pulled through a close-call disaster.

We quickly settled into a pattern. As the stern man, it was my job to steer the boat, keep us on course and safely away from those around us. Rick periodically demanded that we pick up the pace and I provided the commands of "hut" to switch paddling sides. We slowly moved up as we crossed the four miles of the lake. By the time we reached the Vermillion River and our first portage, we were in sixth place and some distance ahead of the boats behind us.

The semi-darkness of the first portage made it difficult to see and we barely missed the large boulders under the water as we struggled to find a landing spot. On shore, we grabbed the life preservers, paddles and canoe and ran the portage as fast as possible.

It quickly became obvious that being in the back and running with the canoe at my waist would not work. With the canoe down and still dark, I was unable to see the narrow path which was crammed with rocks and tree roots as it went steeply up and down. We banged the canoe into trees as we stumbled along. My tennis shoes squished with every step, and the canteen on my waist dangled loose against my soaking wet baggy pants. I was certain I looked like a clown.

Eventually we learned from our mistakes. We buckled the life preservers in the canoe and had Rick carry it, as I managed the rest of the equipment. The rest of the portages went better.

Back in the water, Rick continued to push our pace with periodic demands to "pick it up at the count of 20." He then recognized the Canadians ahead of us who had previously been out of sight, and his competitiveness exploded! There came more demands to "pick it up." Gasping for air, I reminded him that he was 30 years old and I was nearly dead at 52. At the next portage however, it appeared we could pass them. Frantically, we landed and began our run. Rick was in a zone focused entirely on passing the Canadians. But as hard we pushed they beat us to the put-in location. Moments later, we reached it only to have Rick slip on a rock and fall into the water as we launched the canoe. The cold water dampened his fire a bit as he dragged himself out.

Following the last portage, the river opened up and a new challenge confronted us: a gray fog hung over the water which made it, at times, impossible to see the shoreline. Only the tops of the evergreens were visible in the morning light. Drifting into it, we were unsure which way to head. A brief period of stunning silence surrounded us. At one point, we caught a glimpse of our Canadian nemesis disappear into the heavy fog. Uncertain, but thankful for the moment of rest, the silent beauty and the mystery of the fog, we followed them, hoping they were headed in the right direction.

After 15 miles of hard canoeing and portaging, the transition point loomed ahead. At Bucyk bridge, Dave and Rick took over the canoe. They would begin paddling the dreaded "snake pit," a grueling and seemingly endless section of the river.

In the van, Chuck and I drove through deep woods down Fire Road 601. At the end of the road, we came upon the river and a small log cabin named Finn Camp. We settled in and watched two teams pass, followed by the Canadians in third. Thirty minutes later Dave and Rick appeared at the river bend, ecstatic to find us where we were supposed to be.

I climbed back in the canoe with Dave, and took on the second half of the snake pit. After that, it was only a few miles to the last transition.

At the transition point Rick and I re-teamed to make the final push to Crane Lake. We did what we could to catch the Canadians but they drove as fast and as hard in their canoe as they did on their bikes. We weren't able to pass them, but, in the end, we were grateful how they inspired us. Throughout the race, they were our incentive, a goal which enabled us to push harder and maintain our efforts. It was what we needed to face setbacks and persevere on the run and canoe; they energized us to get back to the start line again and again.

Once in Crane lake we picked up the pace to finish strong. As we rounded a bend in the shoreline, we saw the orange flags of the finish and heard the announcer call out our team name. And per tradition, we rolled the canoe and collapsed into the icy waters of Crane Lake.

After drying out, we toasted ourselves with burgers and beer at a nearby resort basking in our accomplishment and reflecting upon the race. In four days with a total racing time of 34 hours, 11 minutes and 10 seconds, our team had come from the flat prairie land of Southwestern Minnesota to its north woods and "land of sky blue waters." Team Red Wing finished fourth out of thirty teams overall and second in the three person division. Whatever individual goals we may have had were overshadowed by five friends sharing efforts to accomplish a test of endurance and resilience.

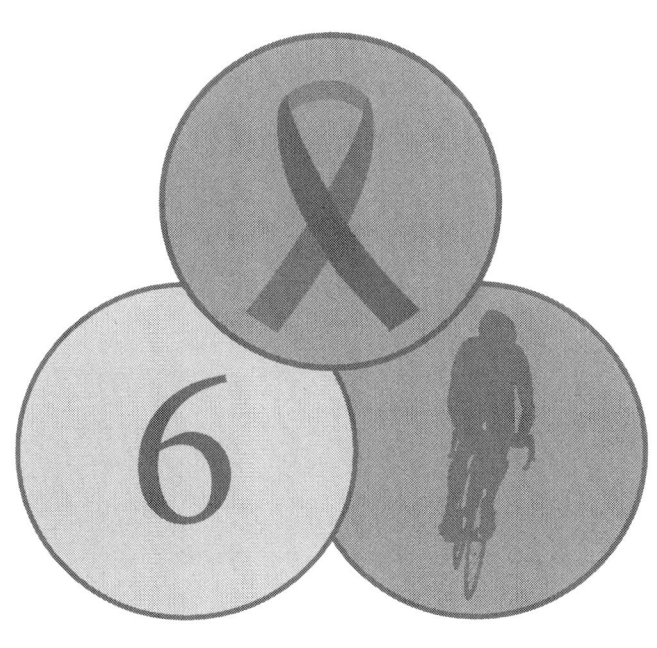

Surgery
and
Radiation

My cancer journey was going to be an easy 5K, a short jog before getting back to living my life. This was my thinking when Kathie and I met with an ENT surgeon in May of 2014. As we discussed surgery to clear the biopsy margins and assess lymph nodes near the site, I figured we were close to the finish line.

A few days later, we arrived early for my surgery. They took me by wheelchair to a room where I put on a hospital gown and sat otherwise naked for a considerable period of time. A nurse inserted an IV needle in my left hand so it would be ready to use when in surgery. Feeling vulnerable already, this did not build my confidence. After a couple of hours, they wheeled me to a larger room where I continued to wait with other patients.

Eventually a nurse approached me, not to bring me back for surgery but to inform me that they would be doing a lymph node scan of my head. This would help the surgeon know the exact location of the lymph nodes - but it did nothing to help my anxiety.

The other patients were not spring chickens. Many sat in wheelchairs, others laid in beds and some looked very ill. My mind drifted back to only three months earlier; I had been at the start line of the Los Angeles Marathon with 20,000 other athletes. Five months before that, I was at the start line for the World Championship Half-distance IRONMAN® triathlon standing shoulder to shoulder with athletes from all over the world in superb physical condition. The stark difference boggled my mind and dramatized how quickly life can change.

As an athlete prepares mentally for a competition, it is important for a patient to mentally prepare for surgery. I had been using a meditation program I'd developed in my work as a psychologist. The program consists of a relaxation method combined with positive suggestions regarding the medical team's skill and expertise, the importance of patient participation in the process and a visualization rehearsal of the surgery with positive outcomes (i.e. faster recovery, less days in the hospital, and little to no pain medication). It is important to practice the program repeatedly two weeks before the procedure. Practice strengthens the suggestions and visualization within our brain so that a positive surgical outcome can be greatly enhanced.

Hearing that I would be receiving a lymph node scan of my head, my claustrophobic anxiety began to rear its ugly head. After they moved me to the scan location, I immediately started using my relaxation method. It helped, and I was blessed further to have a tech assistant who discussed marathons with me. She instructed me to lay down and place my head in the small tube, but I was happily distracted informing her that the 15 marathons I had run had all been in 15 different locations. I told her that after realizing the effort involved in running my first marathon, the 1989 Grandma's in Duluth, I made a vow to always find a new venue if I attempted any others. Thirteen years after Grandma's I ran my second, the beautiful Twin Cities Marathon. Amazingly, though still a novice with a lot to learn, I qualified for the 2003 Boston Marathon at that race.

As the scan process continued, my anxiety lessened. My mind became absorbed in those early running experiences. Being a novice runner at the Twin Cities Marathon, I ran for three to four miles alongside a woman who I thought knew an enormous amount of people. I figured she was either a celebrity or had an extremely large family as everyone was calling her name as she smiled, waved and gave high fives. After a few miles, I was thoroughly convinced she was either a local newscaster or actress until I turned to see she had printed her name on her shirt in large letters.

This seemed like a good idea so, for the Boston Marathon, I printed my name large and bold on my shirt. Sure enough, I started my run and spectators were yelling my name. It was great at first, but that Minnesota Nice thing came into play; every time someone said my name, I needed to acknowledge them back. My head hurt from swiveling to see who knew me. Finally, after a few miles of this, I told myself I was a stranger in a strange city. I knew no one and no one knew me. This worked fine until later someone yelled out my name like it was a question: "Dave?" I kept strong and kept looking straight ahead, but he yelled again, louder, "Dave?!" And my head snapped around to search another crowd of complete strangers. He got me.

The lymph node scan finished around noon and Kathie and I began another wait. About 4:00 p.m., they brought me to the pre-operating room to meet my anesthesiologist. Soon my surgeon and his assistant arrived and they personally wheeled me to the operating room. My surgeon's mood was upbeat and I told him how impressed I was that he had been in surgery all day, but was wide awake and energetic. With a smile, he told me that this was his love and that he had yet another surgical procedure to perform after he was finished with me!

The surgery went well but the biopsy of the lymph nodes found a speck of cancer. This was not what Kathie and I wanted to hear. It was supposed to be a quick 5K run. Still, I was hopeful they would remove it, and two days later I returned for the lymph node surgery.

Because of cancer in two lymph nodes, I qualified for radiation therapy. As a competitor, I'm usually excited for qualifying, but not that time. Kathie and I met the radiation oncologist who told me I would need five treatments several days apart over the course of two weeks. The only side effect would be permanent hair loss in the back of my head. He also stated that I would be fitted with a mask to immobilize my head during the treatment. Neither of these revelations pleased me. Vain perhaps, but I enjoyed longer hair and the idea of a mask fired up my claustrophobia. When I told him of my anxiety he said they could give me 5mg of sedation.

Unfortunately, the 5mg of sedation I had weeks earlier for the PET Scan hadn't lowered my anxiety a whole lot. I wondered if a couple of beers work just as well.

The consultation soured my mood. Arriving home and getting out of my car I accidentally hit the top of my head which was still sore from surgery. "Shit! Dammit!!" My anger spilled out in curse words and it felt good. I was pissed off at this cancer that barged in, took center stage, interrupted my life and affected my family. "Dammit!"

A few days later I went for my first run since surgery, a routine five and half mile route over the noon hour. It not only felt great to be active again but felt especially good to release the pent up anger and fear.

But a week later Kathie and I were back at the clinic to prepare for my radiation sessions. The waiting area at Desk R was crowded when we arrived early in the morning. After being called back by the technician, my head was fitted with a fabric mesh that would be covered by a substance which would harden by the afternoon. The mask covering my head would ensure complete immobility and assist in exact placement of the radiation beams. Once completed, Kathie and I went out for lunch while the mask hardened.

I returned in the afternoon to use the now firm mask while receiving a brain scan. Again, my anxiety soared. The supportive technicians told me to raise my hand if I needed assistance at any time during the procedure. They instructed me to lay on a table, then placed the mask over my head and strapped it down. It was extremely tight, pressing hard on my face and digging into my cheekbones. I was unable to fully open my eyes and I couldn't move my head one iota. As fast as the technicians clamped my head down my hand rocketed up. After getting the mask off me, I told them it was exceedingly tight and my anxiety sky high.

They tried to reassure me, saying such a reaction was common, but then proceeded to re-clamp the mask and my head back onto the table. So much for the break! I closed my eyes and concentrated on relaxing as my head was moved into the confined brain scan machine. Realizing I had five of these to get through wasn't comforting. Perhaps I should have had that beer. Or maybe three.

Leaving the radiation area, I received an intervention from God. Kathie and I met a former secretary. She was there with her husband who had been diagnosed with mouth cancer (although he never smoked, chewed tobacco or drank). Sitting in a wheelchair, he told us he would need daily radiation treatments with the mask Monday through Friday for six weeks. My heart went out to him and suddenly my own treatment worries were put in perspective.

Recognizing I wasn't the only patient suffering with anxiety from this radiation procedure, I wrote and recorded (and used myself) a mental preparation CD of relaxation strategies and positive thoughts. I gave copies to the Radiation Department hoping my experience might assist other patients with anxieties similar to mine.

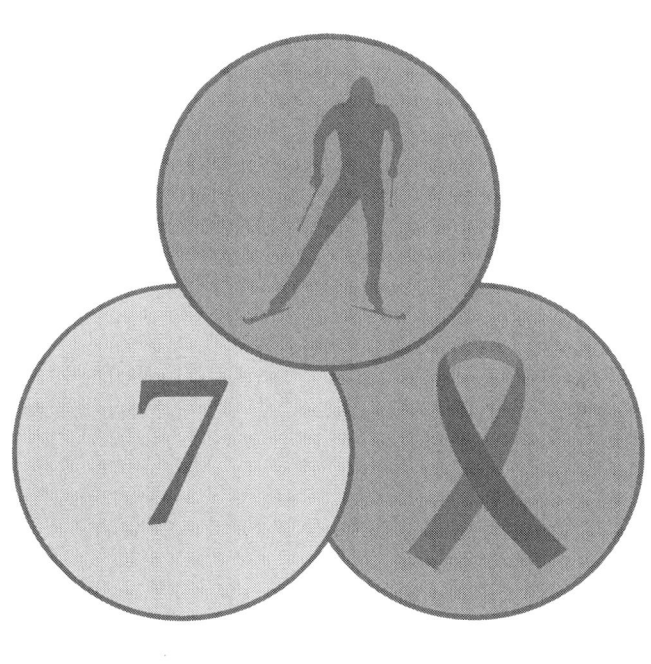

Birkie Fever

My interest in cross country skiing was slow to begin. In fact, after a seven hour ordeal skiing the American Birkebeiner in 1982 I was all but convinced to put away my skis for good. By 1988, however, the race called me back and for the past 28 years I've been skiing the event. When "Birkie Fever" took hold, it helped establish a life style change, spawned a host of new friends, new experiences and eventually was the stimulus to coach high school kids in cross country skiing.

This chapter is centered around my participation in the 1993 American Birkebeiner ski race. After struggling for years in the back waves, this was the year I had made it to first wave placement. I was determined through years of hard work to prove I had the right to be with the faster skiers. From my years involved with the Birkie, I learned the value of preparation, persistence, setting goals and working towards them.

It was early and semi-dark in the cabin as I quietly rummaged through two athletic bags. I didn't want to wake Kathie but I needed appropriate clothes to wear on my trek. The wood stove kept me warm as I wondered why the items I needed were always the hardest to find. Finally, in frustration (but as silently as possible) I dumped everything out of the bags and onto the floor.

At last I was dressed and before the sun rose behind the empty fields I was in the car and on my way. I drove north from our Wisconsin cabin with hope in my heart, but the landscape was bleak, all browns and gray. It was December 16th and this wasn't right, particularly this far north. I had logged enough miles running, cycling and roller skiing; it was almost race season.

I needed to find snow.

In Hayward the winter sun lit the sky but didn't lift my spirits, nor (and more to the point) did it reveal any snow. Besides an occasional clump of dirty slush from a two-week-old storm, there was nothing but dirt and dried up leaves. At a remote county intersection, someone had scattered 30 to 40 of those large inflatable cartoon character Christmas ornaments in a haphazard way over his yard. Without snow, the mass of wires connecting these lumps of plastic were clearly visible in the brown grass. It looked more like a madman's nightmare than a holiday display. I couldn't help thinking, *If this guy isn't on medicine, he should be.*

Farther north I passed the turn off for County OO but there was still no snow. According to the forecast, today's temperature would hit 40 degrees. Was this global warming? Were the animals as bewildered as I was? I wanted to stop the car, walk in the woods, find a bear or a deer or an elk, maybe sit a whole group of them down, and apologize. I wanted to tell them I loved snow and winter too and was ashamed of what we humans were doing to our planet. I wanted them to nod their understanding and tell me it would be okay.

Two more hours I drove north until I found the first smattering of snow. Was it enough to ski on? Probably not. I had one last hope; the farther north I went, the closer I'd come to Lake Superior which often produces lake effect snow.

In the town of Mellen, I drove over old railroad tracks, past the sawmill just out of town and then up the long hill as the road straightened out towards the old mining towns of Iron Belt, Pence, Montreal and Hurley. Finally, only 20 miles from the big lake, significant amounts of the white stuff started to pile up around me. As I drove to the little town of Montreal, past the historic miner homes lining the street, a fresh brilliant white snow covered the trees. I was completely thrilled, totally delighted! Soon, I crossed the state line into Ironwood, Michigan and by 10:00 a.m. I was at the Active Backwoods Retreat Center pushing off with poles and skis on a trail perfectly covered with snow.

Cross country skiers are an odd bunch. We ski long distances in subzero temperatures wearing little more than a thin layer of lycra tights. We tolerate constantly changing variables such as weather, trail grooming and snow conditions, all for a moment of unparalleled skiing. Sometimes, standing for hours in the cold as my eyelashes freeze together, it feels more like a virus than a sport.

Before my life transition, no one would have guessed that I'd be a cross country skier who would awake in the early morning and drive hundreds of miles to find snow. Nor would anyone have guessed that I'd be spending large amounts of money on skis, poles, special clothing and wax. So, what happened? How did I get this infliction?

It all began because of a man named Roger Wistrcill. A natural athlete, he was a teacher, coach and principal at the high school in Cumberland, Wisconsin. He was also my friend and neighbor. In 1979 he told me he had been skiing the American Birkebeiner. While I knew nothing about cross country skiing he encouraged me to try it out and possibly do the race.

Birkebeiner history starts in 1206 when two Birkebeiner skiers, called as such because of protective birch bark leggings, skied through Norway's mountains carrying the infant son of King Sverresson to safety. At that time, Norway was engaged in a civil war between the Birkebeiners and the rebel Bagler forces. After King Sverresson died in 1204, the Bagler forces attempted to find his infant son as they knew he threatened their chances for power. After the young prince subsequently became King of Norway, the two Birkebeiner skiers became a symbol of courage, perseverance and character in the face of adversity. The story of the flight was the inspiration for the first Birkebeiner ski race held in Norway in 1932.

The American Birkebeiner or "Birkie" began in 1973 as the dream of the late Tony Wise, a local entrepreneur and developer of Telemark Lodge in Cable, Wisconsin. Thirty four men and one woman, all clad in woolen sweaters and knickers, competed over a 55 kilometer race from the Lumberjack Bowl in Hayward to Telemark Lodge in Cable. This small group of enthusiasts probably didn't realize they were making history, but that first event would grow to become North America's largest cross country ski marathon which now attracts over 10,000 participants annually.

From its modest beginning, the Birkie became a legend in the cross country ski world surviving cancellation, extreme cold, heavy snowfall, icy trails, thaws and rains. Once skiers are afflicted with "Birkie Fever" they come back year after year. The American Birkebeiner is also a part of the World Loppet circuit of 15 international ski marathons and is included in the American Ski Marathon series of 13 races. The Birkie course is considered to be one of the toughest on the World Loppet circuit as it spans 55 hilly kilometers.

In the early years of the race, participants used the 'classic' or

'stride' technique. Striding is the traditional method where skiers
stay in a track and propel themselves forward with a kicking and
gliding motion. In later years, it became more popular for skiers
to push their legs outward, using a hockey-type motion called the
skating method.

My first experience with the Birkie was in 1979. I had trained

very little and didn't even know how
long a kilometer was, but with Wistrcill's encouragement I decided to ski
the shorter Korteloppet race (half the
distance of the Birkie).

I found the start line for the
"Kortie" at the bottom of a downhill
ski run at the Telemark Lodge and Ski
resort in Cable. When the gun went
off the skiers around me charged like
madmen heading up the downhill ski
slope. I followed, pushing hard, but it
was herringbone (moving with skis
in a V form) all the way to the top.
I tried to stay in a line behind skiers
and not cross skis, but others nearby
stepped on poles or fell, which caused
a chain reaction behind them. With
all this going on, it seemed like an
eternity to get to the top.

The other side was a steep downhill. Even seasoned cross-country
skiers have trouble skiing downhill,

1982 Birkie

so for me as a novice, it was a disaster
waiting to happen. Around me, the
hill was filled with broken poles and a lot of swearing as many
crashed and others ran into them. From the beginning of my descent, I snowplowed to keep my speed under control, but gravity
was relentless. Several times I was forced to use the less elegant
method of riding my butt in the snow.

Finally, I floundered my way around the pileups to the bottom and found the trail into the woods. I had traveled less than a kilometer, but it felt like a whole event had just occurred. I was completely worn out and the woods seemed to go on forever. The rest of the race passed in a blur, but eventually I arrived at the finish line.

It was not a good experience. For weeks my body ached in parts I didn't know I had. Certainly, the Fever hadn't bitten me and I was more dubious than ever about cross country skiing. The whole thing seemed like a lot of work just to "walk" around in the cold.

But somehow, against my better judgement, I decided to ski the full 55 kilometer Birkie in 1982. I must have been a slow learner! Having skied the Korteloppet and now registered for double the distance race, it didn't occur to me that serious training would be a good idea. So, I skied a few times on a golf course and found myself at the Birkie start line in no better shape than I'd been the first time. The gun went off and the race over the next seven hours, became an ordeal. It wasn't pretty, certainly not pleasant and became in the end something more like a death march.

When it was over, I didn't care to ever see another pair of cross country skis again. I left the north woods of Wisconsin and headed south determined to focus my attention off skiing and onto a new job as a psychologist in Red Wing, Minnesota.

So why, six years later, did I change my mind? In part, I remembered Wistrcill's encouragement and knew he continued to ski the Birkie. I also missed the north woods and had started becoming more active. But most importantly, the legend of the race and its symbol of courage and perseverance inspired me. It reminded me that facing adversity head on often leads to triumph and strength.

This time however, I learned from my mistakes. After the 1982 disaster, I knew I needed to train both physically and mentally. I put in the miles and focused on improving my technique. I found others with a passion for the sport and learned from them. When race day came, I thought I was ready.

Unfortunately, the year of my return, the Birkie turned out to be a particularly difficult and cold race (high of five degrees under sunny skies). Without clouds to hold the heat, the temperature barely crawled into positive digits. I had concentrated on my technique and conditioning, but I had not focused enough on my gear. My clothing was not up to the challenge and I came dangerously close to hypothermia before the race was over.

At that point, I had skied a total of three ski races. All them were difficult; and none of them fun.

It would have been easy to again hang up my skis, but some deep part of me wouldn't allow it. I became more determined than ever to master and enjoy this activity. Despite the string of fiascos, I decided to get myself back to the start line. I refused to let three adverse experiences negatively affect my attitude and behavior. So I signed up again the next year, and the year after that. It took some time, but eventually I came down with a case of Birkie fever, and for 28 years I made my annual pilgrimage to northern Wisconsin.

For the 1989 Birkie, my start (based on previous race times) was back in the 6th wave. This put me with mostly recreational skiers and first timers. Racing behind thousands of others, I knew the trail would be deteriorated by the time I got on it. I knew that lines of cautious skiers hesitating on the steep downhills would constantly slow me down. I could hear the announcer start each wave and watched as the barriers opened and skiers took off on the course ahead of me. My frustration grew the longer I waited until finally I made a decision. I would do everything I could to qualify for the first wave.

This desire to be with the faster skiers confirmed a flourishing infliction of the Fever. It took a few years to percolate but when it did, my life changed forever.

To qualify for first wave placement I needed to improve my technique and accumulate as many ski kilometers each season as I could. With the help from Ahvo Taipale, owner of FinnSiSu and others, I improved my skate skiing ability and made many trips in search of snow and groomed trails. Sometimes they would be short trips to local places like St. Mary's College in Winona, or Willow River State Park in Hudson, Wisconsin. And sometimes I'd make the four and half hour drive to Ironwood, Michigan to ski three hours and return the same day.

Many of my trips were with friend, Bob Alleva. This was a man whose drive brought him in only a few years to reach his goal: qualifying for the Birkie Elite Wave, the top 200 skiers. The two of us traveled to many races together including the Pepsi Challenge and the Noequamenon ski race in Marquette, Michigan. Alleva had a way of making every event an adventure.

One year, several of us struggled to decide whether or not we were going to drive five hours north in January for the Pepsi Challenge in Biwabik, Minnesota. For a number of years, I had skied it as it was a reliable training race for the Birkie. The problem this year? The forecast for Saturday's race called for subzero weather. Even though I needed the training, I hesitated at the thought of cold skiing and worried we would drive all the way to find the race had been cancelled. After a long deliberation, one of the guys said, "What? Are we wimps? Let's go!"

It was a long ride in Bob's cargo van. It had a horrible defrosting mechanism and for five hours we were encased in a cocoon of window frost. It was frigid cold and late when we reached Biwabik. I headed to Kenny K's Bar to pick up the key for the house we rented. We quickly found that while the rent was cheap and it had heat, the place was old and smelled of mold and cigarette smoke. Discolored wallpaper peeled from the wall and the once white lace window drapes were now a sickly yellow. Despite the surroundings we each found a place to sleep to get ready for the next day's 50 kilometer race.

In the morning, after scraping frost off the window, I made out chimney exhaust streaming from nearby houses. Alleva, who had been to race headquarters told us, "It's 30 below zero."

"You're kidding?" I said, but unfortunately, he was not. He told us the race had been delayed from an 8:00 to 10:00 a.m. start in hopes for warmer temperatures. By 10:00 a.m. it was 18 below so race officials delayed the start another hour and shortened the race to 25 kilometers. Temperatures held steady at 18 below making the start bone-chilling and the snow on the course slower than molasses (cold snow is like sand with minimal glide). We trudged through the race and finished, but it was the last time any of us skied the Pepsi Challenge in January.

Training trips were not without their moments of reflection and poignancy. On one trip, I unexpectedly met Bob Alleva in Ironwood. Alleva lived in Red Wing but was visiting his mother who lived in the family home nearby. As I was stowing my skis in the car, Alleva asked what I was doing for lunch. I had no plans so Bob told me to visit his Mom in nearby Hurley, as she would have food ready. I hesitated. Bob wouldn't be there and it felt odd for me to walk in alone and expect her to feed me. Bob assured me that as she has done most of her life, his mom had spent most of her mornings preparing food and it would be just fine.

Somewhat reluctantly, I drove the few miles to Hurley, Wisconsin. On Fifth Street, I passed the high school football field which promoted: "Home of the Fighting Midgets." A few blocks later I reached the Alleva home. I knocked on the door and Bob's mother, Polly, greeted me warmly. The smell of red sauce and garlic filled the home. I apologized and told her Bob insisted I come. But she took it in stride and just treated me like one of her kids coming home for lunch. She invited me to the table and offered salad with vinegar and oil dressing, gnocchi, meat and cheese ravioli, and homemade pasta with red sauce and meat balls.

A Polish woman, Polly married Bob's father who was Italian and worked in the local silver mines. As a part of their nuptial agreement, Bob's father had insisted Polly spend the year prior to the wedding with his Italian mother learning the traditional ways of Italian cooking. The fruits of her commitment were evident as I enjoyed every bite of my Italian lunch. But it wasn't the food alone that made the moment so special. Certainly, the generosity of Bob and his mother was a part of it, but sitting in Polly's kitchen reminded me of watching my mother bake and prepare meals.

My mother was my rock and was taken too soon from this life. She left this earth without ever knowing all of her grandchildren, but she's never been far from my mind. Diagnosed with cancer of the pancreas, she died at age 62, after fighting a long, difficult battle. In that moment in Polly's kitchen, I remembered my mother's strength and deepened my resolve to reach my goals. It's what she would have wanted.

After all the training and trips to find snow, I came to the 1993 American Birkebeiner prepared for the challenge. I woke early on the morning of the race. It was cold as I prepared a drink mix of coffee and Exceed in my water bottle. I'd drink it at the 48 kilometer mark in the hope it would power me through to the finish.

The Birkie is a point to point race so most participants have to be bused from various locations to the start. To manage this, the Birkie organization operates one of the largest bus systems in the state on race day. It is efficient, but given some 10,000 participants, it is critical to plan ahead and leave extra time to get to the start.

In the dark, cold morning I found a seat on a school bus crowded with fellow skiers and their gear. I had gotten on an early bus to insure a good placement in my wave. The start line was near the small airport adjacent to Telemark Lodge which was where the bus dropped us off. Once off the bus, I took refuge in the lodge to stay warm before the final walk to the chute entrance of my wave. In

The start of the American Birkebeiner

the hour before the start I managed to eat a PowerBar which, when added to the pasta carbo-loading the night before, should get me through the race.

Around 7:45 a.m. I walked the half mile to the start. Clouds covered the sun, making it feel even colder than eight below. Walking didn't seem to generate much heat and I already started burning precious calories to keep warm. With half an hour to go, I faced one of the most difficult parts of the race. I regretfully pull off my warm up clothes and stuffed them in a bag which I handed to a volunteer at the clothes bag truck. Despite the cold morning, the volunteers were friendly. They handle thousands of bags and, unlike the airlines, they have never lost one.

Without warm up clothes I kept moving to get myself to the Wave One chute area. The start procedure involved two successive pens, each of which was separated by a gate (a series of rope work which was raised and lowered by volunteers). When a wave started, each pen gate would open, allowing skiers to move up as fast as they were able (if they want a good position) to the next gate. The wait at the chute entrance seemed long but, on the bright side, standing in a tight group of other skiers helped block the icy wind. Finally, the chute opened and we stampeded toward the starting line. At this point we were on foot, running with poles and skis in hand as we jockeyed for a position.

I made it to the first line standing shoulder to shoulder with more than five hundred other skiers. The course stretched in front of us and thousands of others waited behind us in various waves. The Elite Wave (Men & Women) had already left and only minutes remained until my start.

I couldn't help reflecting on the magnitude of my position. After my first Birkie, I never wanted to see another pair of cross country skis again. Then after a lot of encouragement, I found myself in the sixth wave looking at thousands of skiers in front of me. At that time, I promised myself I would work to qualify for the first wave. Finally, after years of training, I stood in the first row of the first wave.

I struggled to hold back emotions. I had made it. I had achieved my goal and I thought of those who helped me accomplish it. Now I needed to focus on the next goal: prove to myself that I belonged there.

As the clock ticked to two minutes left, a woman next to me struggled with the draw string on her tights. To my shock, she then pulled her tights down and with 4,000 mostly male skiers behind her, she squatted to pee on the snow. Amazingly, this didn't take long and within seconds of getting her tights and poles back in place, the start gun went off.

The barricade lifted and skiers furiously double poled to get to the front. Like an old western movie where thousands of soldiers on horseback clashed with thousands of Indians, the crowd surged forward. Many poles broke and skiers piled up in a mess of limbs. Fortunately for many, volunteers offered substitute poles along the first few kilometers for those who needed them.

After the first 100 yards, skiers began to skate and I was thrilled to know I made the right decision on wax as my skis glided well. To get ahead of slower racers, I pushed hard but carefully so as not to fall for fear of being trampled by the stampede of crazed skiers behind me.

As we rounded Telemark Lodge the crowd began to thin and I hadn't fallen or been stabbed by a pole. So far, so good. After three kilometers the trail narrowed and with hundreds of skiers coming through, it created a log jam. Someone yelled, "Double pole!" but I was too slow to respond and within seconds I was down and inter-twined in skis that were not mine. A stumble, but I leapt up as fast as I had gone down. After a quick check to confirm I had broken no poles, skis or bones, I pushed ahead.

The Powerline section of the trail followed a series of major hills gaining 400 feet over the next two kilometers. The pace was exceedingly fast and by the first feed station, I had already become exhausted. But Birkie volunteers greeted me in a friendly, upbeat mood and their excitement reenergized me as the trail ducked into the woods.

For the next 45 kilometers, the course followed a series of rolling hills interspersed with five major climbs. I settled into a reasonable pace as the field continued to thin. Eventually, I reached the infamous Bobblehead Hill, a curvy, tricky descent. Every year many (usually inebriated) snowmobilers gathered to cheer and jeer at those who fall. When a skier bit the dust they'd hold up numbers like Olympic judges. Fortunately, I descended without incident.

Near the halfway mark, a skier appeared at my side like a skeleton out of a closet. She said, "There you are, I've been trying to catch up but my boot got unbuckled." I gasped. It was the woman next to me at the start! Completely surprised I mumbled something like, "Have a good ski," as she sped past me.

A little further, near County OO, and 27 kilometers into the course, the Kortelopet skiers (those doing half the course) finished their race. I was feeling strong and the crowd of people ringing their Birkie bells at this point encouraged me.

Over the next ten kilometers, I passed a significant number of skiers and felt good pushing on to the Mosquito Brook feed zone at 39 kilometers. At the feed zone, however, my mood changed. Each hill seemed like a mountain. My pace slowed and my legs and arms began to ache with every stroke. I took a moment to eat a couple of doughnut holes and orange slices. As I skied away, I pulled out my water bottle and took a swig of my secret weapon, coffee and lime-flavored Exceed. It tasted god-awful but in the name of competition, I choked it down.

After Mosquito Brook, I faced a long gradual climb ending with a series of rollers cumulating with the steep climb up "Bitch Hill." There women at the top dressed as "bitches" cheered and tossed Mardi Gras beads. I was out of breath and in no mood to acknowledge their encouragement. Fortunately, I had two long down hills to recover.

As I approached the crossing at Highway 77, it became a survival race to the finish. I pushed up one last long climb then followed a sweeping downhill into the final two kilometers across Lake Hayward. Once on the lake, it began to lightly snow and skiers stretched silently across the wide expanse of the frozen landscape. Exhausted, we made our way down Main Street through the cheering crowds and the finish.

Even though the glory in a competitive event typically goes to the top athletes and winners, it has become clear to me that the real spirit of a race is often not at the front but with those at the back. I have been there and know the suffering that is experienced.

In 1997, I crossed the finish line around noon after having started three hours earlier. As usual, my wife, Kathie, was among thousands of spectators and family members waiting near the finish for racers to cross. After it was over, we hung around at the clothes bag area, then the food tent. We met friends, talked with others and then drove 30 miles back to Cable near the start of the race. There, I showered, changed and socialized at a friend's cabin. By late afternoon, I had had a few beers and was exhausted.

We left the party and drove through the cold and dark back to Hayward. As we rolled into town, a couple of snow plows were moving into position to clear off Highway 63 (snow is dumped on Hwy 63 so that racers can cross onto Main Street). Slowly motoring around the detour, we saw the last few Birkie skiers coming off Lake Hayward and heading toward Main Street. The street was empty of spectators except for a few cheering friends and family members - who themselves had been standing in the cold for hours ringing their Birkie bells and waiting for their skier to make his/her appearance.

I had been there. I remember struggling in after six to seven hours on a brutally cold day, having faced one of the world's most challenging trails. Those last Birkie skiers experienced in those late hours a smattering of support. It wasn't as loud as it had been for the first finishers, but each cheer was enormously important to help get them to the finish line. It was a dramatic show of what the Finnish people call SISU which means toughness, resiliency, determination and courage.

In August 2016 Roger Wistrcill, the man who introduced me to the Birkebeiner, turned 70 years old. He had been battling stage four colon cancer for six years but demonstrated courage and resiliency as he continued to participate in "Birkie Week" in Hayward. Kathie and I helped celebrate his birthday at his home on Beaver Dam Lake in Cumberland, Wisconsin. Family and friends were in attendance, many of whom had also been bitten by the Fever as a result of Roger's encouragement. One of those friends, Mike Clay, shared with us a poem that he wrote:

TO LIFE, THE BIRKIE, AND SEVENTY YEARS
By Mike Clay

We foolishly took to the race
With very little knowledge or skill
We skied with our hearts and not much else
When we finished we'd had our fill.

For reasons I can't explain
Maybe a fever that wouldn't let go
We returned to the race again and again
Strapped on skis and took to the snow.

Somewhere along the journey
As we skied the long trail to the end
The race was transformed into tales and stories
That all started, "Remember when…"

And that is what we take with us
Long after the ski race ends
We measure that trail not in K's or miles
But in stories told between friends

Now we turn seventy, a ripe old age
When the tales get muddled and fade
But the race is true and calls to you
And the stories that are still to be made.

Broken Poles

After my surgery and radiation, I was considered cancer free. This, of course, validated my previous thinking that this journey would be a short 5K run. Now I just needed to recover from the treatments and my life would be back in order. Following radiation, I had a prolonged sore throat and my taste buds were severely affected. As the saying goes, you don't know what you have until you lose it. The loss of taste, particularly the taste of sweet, was extremely difficult. Over time it contributed to a mild level of depression.

But two months later, my taste buds returned to normal, the sore throat was long gone and, happily, I had not experienced any hair loss on the back of my head. There was no evidence of disease and I felt good about my health. Things were looking up so I convinced my friend David Roseen to register with me for the Ogden Marathon in the spring.

Only a few months after that, however, the brightness of being cancer free dimmed when small bumps appeared on the back of my head. With a feeling of dread, I made an appointment with my doctor. Sure enough, biopsies revealed malignant melanoma. To make matters worse, I went through a PET Scan assessment for melanoma around the same time. It showed my PSA was within normal limits, but the scan revealed cancer in my prostate gland.

In a matter of weeks, I went from cancer free to having two different cancers occupying my body. Shocked by this news, I lost any illusions I had of this being a quick fix. I attempted to use humor to cope. "Two cancers for the price of one," I'd say. And, "How many more cancers are in there?" But inside, both Kathie and I were alarmed.

For the melanoma, my dermatologist suggested a relatively new chemotherapy treatment of directly injecting the drug "X" into the melanoma lesions. The treatment had been used in Europe and the clinic was only one of few in the country attempting it. My physician had experienced some success with it on other patients. Though the treatment was uncommon, I had full trust in my dermatologist, and agreed to try it.

I showed up at the clinic every three days for four weeks. Each session, they gave me a choice between two, three or four vials of the drug. Each vial consisted of three to five injections directly into my lesions. If I chose fewer vials per session, it lengthened the treatment period.

Initially, I could tolerate the sessions, but soon the back of my head became a tender pin cushion with each injection becoming more excruciating. My dermatologist would frequently apologize for the pain. I believe I can tolerate a fair amount, but by the last injection on the last day of treatment, the intense pain brought me to tears. I'm not sure I would have been able to keep showing up if it weren't for Kathie. She went with me to every session. Her presence and support was invaluable.

While I was going through this, I also had to deal with prostate cancer and went to the Urology Department for a biopsy. Whatever modesty I had before that appointment was stripped away as they performed the procedure. Without going into too much detail, let's just say I'll never use a staple gun again.

A few days later they gave me the results. They indicated a Gleason score of seven which related to a medium level of cancer. This meant surgery. As a result, I consulted with my urologist to schedule a procedure to remove the cancer from my prostate. We agreed to December 12th so I could still attend our high school Nordic ski camp.

For nine years I had been an Assistant Coach for the Red Wing high school cross country team. When initially asked by Coach

Jesse Nelson I wasn't sure whether it would be a good fit. My own kids were out of the house and I didn't know if I could relate to teenagers any more. Ultimately, I made the decision to coach primarily so I could teach visualization and performance enhancement skills to young athletes. I also hoped the team's daily practice routines would encourage me to run more often. It didn't take long, however, before I realized what a joy it was to be around these kids. Their energy was contagious.

At the end of the 2010 cross country season, one of the team members asked if I'd be willing to coach him and several other kids in cross country skiing. I was thrilled at the opportunity to share my joy of cross country skiing with others. I made the commitment excited to give back to a sport that has given me so much.

Red Wing Nordic began that year with four high schoolers. Because of them and the support of parents and others, by the fifth year (2015-2016) the team had grown to 31 athletes. We soon established a grade school youth ski development program (the Screaming Eagles) and an annual Nordic ski camp to help participants prepare for the ski season. Through these efforts, cross country skiing grew closer to becoming a high school sport.

With two cancers in me and the Nordic camp looming ahead, I did what I could to cope. I regularly practiced a relaxation/visualization program of imagining my immune system eating up the cancer. This helped reinforce the idea that I had a role in my health. Then, as much as was possible, I maintained my exercise routine of running, cycling, swimming and roller skiing. Kathie and I continued to express our feelings, validating and supporting one another. We kept reminding ourselves we had a treatment plan with one of the world's finest medical facilities. This gave us hope.

I continued to read from the devotional book Bob Goetz gave me. It reminded me God was always with me, providing steadiness when the world is in chaos. Difficulties in life happen and I knew it was important not to run from them. Instead, times like these were opportunities to embrace God's grace, rely more fully on Him and trust that He would bring the good out in all circumstances. When I could do this, negativity lost its grip and problems faded in significance.

Still, I struggled to cope and needed to rely on the support of friends and community. Often that support presented itself when I least expected it.

In many ski races, like the American Birkebeiner, volunteers stood on the sidelines to hand out poles if a competitor broke one. There were skiers who, when you fell at the bottom of a hill, would stop their race to help you out. There were individuals who stood in the cold ringing their cow bell for the last few competitors.

The kids on the Red Wing Nordic team did this for me through my cancer journey. I doubt they ever realized the number of poles they gave me when mine had broken or how many times they were there to help me up when I fell at the bottom of those hills. When things grew dark and it became hard for Kathie and me to see light at the end of the tunnel, the kids with their youthful spirit were out there ringing their bells.

Our Nordic ski camp gave me the energy to face my surgery. The surgery went well with a complete extraction of the cancer. Nancy Olson, another one of my journey's many supportive angels, came to visit as I recovered in the hospital the next day. Trained in Healing Touch, Nancy preformed the technique, infusing me in a deep level of comfort and relaxation. Since that day, she's unselfishly volunteered her time and expertise to help me heal and relax with these techniques.

Recovery from surgery took longer than expected, however, and I experienced prolonged upset stomach, constipation and an altered taste of food. As a result, I wasn't able to concentrate on my training and was disappointed when I had to cancel the trip to the Ogden Marathon.

In March 2015, I underwent another PET Scan to confirm if the surgery had removed all the prostate cancer. The lights of my world dimmed again as the news was not good. While the cancer in the prostrate was gone, the melanoma, once contained, had spread to my liver, bone and spleen. Now with Stage 4 cancer, what I'd previously imagined to be an easy 5K run had turned into a marathon.

Peace in the Storm

We faced nature directly when we skied the secluded back country of Yellowstone National Park. We left the comfort of our routines to breathe, see and feel a power larger than ourselves. We entered the unexplored wilderness and it stirred our souls, awakened our emotions and ultimately deepened our spirits. As Thoreau said, "We need the tonic of the wilderness...we cannot have enough of nature."

This was not a race but a time to experience the peace God provides in nature's wilderness. Jesus often withdrew to the wilderness by himself for reflection and prayer. Getting away from the demands of everyday life, and experiencing God's creation is like walking hand in hand with God. It can provide a serenity to cushion the chaos and uncertainties of life.

We stood alone at the rim of the canyon. The moonlight illuminated the rugged snow-covered walls in black and white. The chasm below us plunged a thousand feet to the churning Yellowstone River, a thin silver ribbon shimmering in the moonlight. Below us we heard a faint roar and above us the night sky glistened with starlight. We had turned off our headlamps to ski by the light of the moon and now, standing underneath the vastness of the heavens at the edge of this great abyss, we savored an extraordinary peace.

Six of us came to ski the backcountry of the Yellowstone wilderness. Several months earlier, Roger Wistrcill, the man who introduced me to the Birkie, had asked if I'd be crazy enough to sign on for this trip. Our friend Mike Clay, English teacher and fellow Birkie skier, was organizing it. Others crazy enough included Jon, a retired airline pilot with Birkie experience; Steve, an attorney with limited cross country ski experience; and Dave, a Colorado radio station consultant with considerable downhill ski experience but little on cross country skis.

From West Yellowstone we shuttled 40 miles by snow coach to the Canyon Yurt Camp, secluded in a small meadow and surrounded by pine forest. Centrally located at an altitude of 8,000 feet, there were no other people or overnight accommodations within 35 miles. All park roads were closed so there was no traffic, no lines of gawking tourists and no RVs. Six feet of snow covered the vacant campgrounds. The few snowmobiles we saw as we entered the park had disappeared. In short, we were perfectly isolated from the world outside.

Preparing for this trip, the thought of losing contact or getting caught in an avalanche had crossed my mind a number of times. Driving in, signs offered stark warnings: 'When you choose to explore Yellowstone, you experience the land on its own terms; there is no guarantee of your safety.' The history of the area abounds with accounts of individuals and small parties lost in the mountains or disorientated in remote canyons. Many have perished in avalanches or blizzards.

Our wilderness camp was near the north rim of what's called The Grand Canyon of the Yellowstone, a 20 mile gorge approximately 1,000 feet deep and up to 4,000 feet wide. At the west end of the canyon, just a short ski away, was Lower Falls, a 308 foot waterfall twice the size of Niagara Falls. Mount Washburn at 10,243 feet was visible to the north.

In the center of camp, two large yurts served as the kitchen and dining area. They were heated by wood stoves and similar to those used by nomadic Mongolian tribes. Surrounding these two main yurts were ten smaller individually heated tents outfitted with either double or single beds. Finally, there was a heated outhouse, shower facility and sauna.

Our backcountry guides were Sarah and David, a young couple from Eugene, Oregon. They proved to be phenomenal workhorses capable of breaking trail through deep snow during the long ski treks.

After breakfast our group travelled four miles by snow coach to the Violet Hot Springs Trailhead on the Canyon/Norris road. Clouds scattered across the early morning sky, the temperature was in the high teens and there was a possibility for strong winds and snow.

We left the security of the snow coach, hooked in our skis and plunged onto the snow-filled track. We would follow it over the rolling forested terrain of the Central Plateau to the northwest side of Hayden Valley.

Our route took us through acres of trees charred by the fires of

1988 although there was plenty of regrowth. The new evergreens seemed small, but the five to six feet of snow we were skiing on made it difficult to estimate their exact size. We crossed several small to medium size meadows on our way to the upper reaches of Otter Creek. Two hours into the route the sky darkened and the wind began to pick up.

Our guide Dave had been breaking trail most of the way. I followed close behind but there was little conversation. The group stretched so I lost sight of those toward the rear. Sarah took the last position to ensure that we would not separate from each other. At one point Dave stopped in a submerged area of forest partially protected from the wind and reported it was just a short distance to Violet Hot Springs and then beyond was the wide clearing of Hayden Valley where the wind would intensify and feel colder.

We continued on. Just before lunch, Dave spotted a coyote climbing a ridge to our right. While I couldn't see the animal, I noticed ravens circling the area where the coyote was heading. Suspecting a dead animal over the rise, Dave skied to its crest. On

Deep in the heart of Yellowstone wilderness

his return, he confirmed that a bison yearling had succumbed to the laws of nature.

After the group had reassembled we searched for a protected place to have lunch. We approached an area that looked to meet our needs but to get there we first needed to navigate a long downhill slope. As I began the descent, my lack of downhill ski ability became immediately apparent. Dodging around trees in deep powder, I crashed landed like a wounded duck. Behind me, Jon followed my tracks down the hill. The retired pilot crouched low - not for aero dynamics but to maintain a shorter distance to fall - and flapped his arms and poles like wings in an attempt to provide balance. Halfway down it became obvious where he'd end up. Amazingly, he pulled out a relatively smooth landing. Before he was off the trail, however, Roger had begun his descent and was heading straight toward Jon. Realizing the danger, Roger tried forcing a turn but his ski caught and it catapulted him forward driving his face deep in the powder. In the process, he lost one of the lens of his dark glasses and for the remainder of the day he looked like Long John Silver with a patch over his eye.

We spent little time on lunch preferring the warmth that came from staying active. Back on skis we headed over a ridge which protected us from the stiff wind. It began to snow and the wind pushed it in our face, each flake stinging us with cold.

For three kilometers we wound through trees and burned timber until we entered an eerie fog produced by steam from the boiling hot springs and light snow. A smell of sulfur hung over everything as we removed our skis and walked through the Violet Hot Springs geyser area. Fifty feet to our right, a lone bison stood motionless in the snow and steam-filled air.

After our time at Violet Hot Springs we turned east into the wide expanse of wilderness known as Hayden Valley. The snow had intensified and gusts of winds caused intermittent whiteouts making it difficult to distinguish the landscape. We attempted to stay together but a number of skiers had dropped farther back.

In the summer I imagine Hayden Valley is a peaceful oasis filled with high prairie grasses and wild flowers stretching to the evergreen forests and then beyond to the snow covered mountains. But on that day, it was a barren landscape in shades of white and gray that most resembled Antarctica. Even though our guide, Dave, was right in front of me, the Valley's wide expanse and the howl of the fierce wind made me feel profoundly alone.

A few kilometers into the Valley we came to Alum Creek, a steaming hot water creek which wound through the valley. Farther downstream a herd of bison were faintly visible through the blowing snow and steam. We gathered together in a submerged area partially protected from the wind. Taking time to re-wax, I heard Roger announce that he decided to immerse himself in the 104 degree water. Had his face plant kilometers ago caused him to go mad? Or was the incessant wind giving me auditory hallucinations?

Moments later, with steam swirling around him, he stepped naked into the warm stream. I quietly prayed for no one to follow, but my heart sank as one by one everyone committed to the hot water soak. Before long, and against my better judgement, I stood on a small, wet rock abandoning the warmth of layered clothing. Quickly I slipped in the hot water just as Sarah emerged from where she had been watching the bison herd.

The natural pool was large enough for all of us to bask in comfort. Minutes before, we had struggled through wind and snow over an Antarctic-like landscape, but now our contented white bodies soaked in a hot tub as if at some posh resort.

The respite was short lived, however, and it was soon time to return across Hayden Valley. I pulled on my clothes at light speed. Then I hooked in my skis and started trudging once again through deep powder. Unrelenting winds had caused the trail to drift over and snow continued to fall. Dave and I soon separated from the group. I was no longer able to see the others as the conditions had isolated us. Ice crystals pelted my face as I pressed forward constantly shifting my weight against the powerful gusts.

Uncertain of where to go, I placed my trust in my guide. Because of the howling wind, Dave said nothing but pointed to a lone tree barely visible in the blowing snow that marked our direction.

Experiencing the enormous power of God's wilderness creation, I felt no fear, but was at peace. As in life, I may not always know where the trail will turn or when it will end; circumstances will look threatening and uncertain; and events will happen that fill in the trail and make it challenging to proceed forward. When this happens, all I can do is step forward in faith, trusting God will provide and bestow strength with his promise of salvation.

Finally, I reached the lone tree. Beyond it, we had a few kilometers left to the Yellowstone River and the pickup point. Dave received a call from Sarah on the two-way radio revealing that one of the skiers was having trouble and requested that we try to widen the trail which would make it easier for him to ski. We did what we could, but, with the wind and drifting snow, much of the trail quickly refilled.

We came over a rise and skied toward the river where the snow coach would pick us up. Dave went back to check on the others as I skied ahead to the road which followed the rushing river.

As I separated from Dave, a coyote appeared along the opposite bank. Away from his pack, he sensed my presence and, with two graceful leaps, he disappeared into the forest.

Skiing along the river canyon provided a refuge from the wind. Large snowflakes fell into perfect silence. I felt the presence of God wrapped around me. I lingered, feeling surrounded by perfect peace, knowing that soon I would need to look for the snow coach to take me home.

Summit
of Hope

The call from my dermatologist on South Oaks Drive announcing my cancer had metastasized to my liver, bone and spleen shook me. I made it to the top of the hill exhausted and anxious to be home. Emotions overwhelmed me as I walked the last block and half. I dreaded telling Kathie. She'd been on the journey with me and would be devastated by the news.

Fortunately, I didn't have long to fret as Kathie unexpectedly drove alongside and stopped the car next to me. Our eyes met and the brightness in her eyes quickly dimmed. After 41 years of marriage she immediately knew something was wrong. Within moments, we were holding each other in the middle of the road sharing the love between us. In her arms, I felt her support and strength and knew I wouldn't face cancer alone.

Kathie and I had some time to process, but within two hours we sat at our living room table listening to my dermatologist on the speaker phone. He had already presented my case to the Oncology Tumor Board at the clinic, (a group of some 50 physicians specializing in cancer), and would be setting up an appointment for me with a melanoma oncologist. He described him as "Dr. Melanoma" and indicated he was one of the foremost oncologists in the world.

I appreciated my doctor's upbeat attitude and tone, but I wasn't optimistic. The 5K run had become a marathon, and I had already had far too many recommendations, doctors and treatments. We hung up the phone, and with hope flickering like a dying candle, I said to Kathie, "We need a miracle."

It was soon to come.

On March 17th I was in the exam room on the 10th floor of the Gonda Building. Kathie is 100% Irish and would be spending her St. Patrick's Day in Rochester next to me. She had been my resident angel throughout the process, but we were about to meet another angel: my new oncologist, Dr. M.

Dr. M hated to lose to cancer. He was committed to finding a cure, and his presence as he entered the room wasn't about Irish luck, it was a blessing. He greeted us cordially and within seconds, his relaxed demeanor, his modesty and friendliness put us at ease.

Bracing for gloomy news, I began our session by stating, "I know things look pretty dismal."

"Dismal?!" he passionately responded. "No. No. Dr. Asp, we have many options and things to offer."

Hearing this, my Irish wife leapt up with tears in her eyes, and threw her arms around him.

Now that he knew us well, Dr. M listed an array of viable and effective treatment programs for metastatic melanoma; these including surgery, targeted therapies, standard chemotherapy and some newly developed immunotherapies.

The immunotherapy was particularly compelling. In a sense, the approach treated the patient and not the tumor. My immune system already knew how to fight the cancer; it just needed a little help. The drugs in this therapy were used to release the brakes on immune cells, making them more effective at killing cancer. Dr. M said it was another weapon to outsmart the cancer and was proving to be effective, especially against melanoma.

I needed a doctor who understood how I felt. I needed a doctor who wouldn't give up or lose hope. I needed a doctor who would fight with me all the way to the conclusion of this journey. Dr. M was exactly who I needed and Kathie and I left the appointment with a plan in place and renewed hope.

A few days later I underwent an ultrasound-guided biopsy of the lesion in my liver. I thought by this time I'd be prepared for any test or procedure they could throw at me, but the liver biopsy was astonishing. They kept me fully alert and had me lie on my back. Then the radiologist, guided by ultrasound, calmly inserted a long needle/tool just under my rib cage and down to my liver. Amazingly, with a little help of pain medication, there was only pressure, no pain. Not surprisingly, the biopsy revealed metastatic melanoma.

Soon, I began four intravenous immunotherapy treatments of drug "A" once every three weeks. Each session lasted two hours and each bag of the drug dripping into my body cost an astounding amount of money. Thankfully, I was blessed to have outstanding medical insurance that would pay these phenomenal costs.

Other than itching, the treatments had no significant side effects and I was able to continue running. In fact, I ran with my daughter, Keri, in the annual Get In Gear 10K race in April.

Incredibly, by the last immunotherapy session, a PET Scan in July revealed no evidence of cancer! A miracle had happened.

I had a hard time believing the news. But Dr. M showed us the PET Scan image of my body and no cancer lights were displayed. Astounded by the power of only four treatments, I asked him if we should do a few more for insurance. He explained that it would not be a good idea as too much of the immunotherapy can be toxic to the body.

Leaving the consultation office, a heavy burden had been lifted off my shoulders. I felt free again. With a hug and kiss, Kathie and I rejoiced and treated ourselves to a dinner out.

It is amazing what a shot of hope can do. I felt an enormous resurgence of energy and convinced my friend, Dave Roseen, to sign up with me for the Madison Marathon in October. Additionally, Kathie's family was ready for another reunion which had started to include a running event.

Several years ago, Kathie's brother John, began competing in marathons. Then her niece Megan, an accomplished college athlete, started to run and wanted to complete a marathon herself. So in 2010 the family held a reunion centered on running the Big Sur Marathon. After Big Sur we did the Moab Marathon in 2011 and then the Los Angeles Marathon in 2014. By that time, the reunion had become a family fixture. In the fall of 2014 we gathered in New York City to run the inspirational Stephen Siller 5K Tunnel To Tower Run commemorating the firefighter's fatal run from Brooklyn to the Twin Towers on 9/11. In looking for locations and courses for the next marathon reunion, we decided to run the San Francisco Marathon in July of 2016. Signed up and feeling good, I assumed my good health would continue.

In the summer of 2015, Kathie and I also attended a Mayo Clinic sponsored patient symposium on melanoma treatment and research. As a result of what we learned and our experience on this cancer adventure, a seed was planted and later germinated when we created a power point presentation and began speaking to school age kids and community groups on the dangers of ultraviolet radiation and skin cancer.

Energized by success and wanting to celebrate my recovered health, I convinced Kathie to accompany me in July to climb the peaks of Route Combo in Colorado. Years ago, I heard about this trail hike in the Rockies where, if one was in good enough shape, he/she could reach the summit of all four mountains in one day. The mountains that form Route Combo are Democrat, Cameron, Lincoln and Bross, each of which exceed 14,000 feet elevation. For years, the image of me hiking up that solitary mountain trail endured, and I was ready to turn my fantasy into reality.

Although it was risky, I planned it as a quick in and out over a long weekend. Weather in the mountains is extremely variable. Even in July, snow, sleet, hail or high winds can shut down any chance of climbing a summit. But we decided to take our chances and make the journey.

Base camp in Colorado was the Fairplay Hotel, a historic building established in 1873 in the little town of Fairplay at a daunting elevation of 9,953 feet. We arrived late afternoon in cold, raw wind conditions. Dark and ominous clouds covered the sky. After checking in, we headed to High Alpine Sports to get weather and trail information and small handheld oxygen canisters for use at high elevations.

The friendly young clerk told us the trail was in good shape and the road to the trailhead was bumpy but passable, even without a high clearance 4WD vehicle. He recommended we begin our hike early so that we could be off the mountain by noon given the possibility of afternoon thunderstorms. Trusting his judgement, Kathie and I went to bed early, and I dreamed of a solitary hike on a remote mountain trail.

At 4:30 the next morning we drove north on Highway 9 from Fairplay to the little town of Alma. In the middle of town on the side of the road, a sign directed us towards the road to Kite Lake and the trailhead.

Initially the dirt road was relatively smooth but the farther we went, the rougher it became. Soon our little Prius was taking huge nose dives into what seemed like road canyons. We jostled as I attempted to navigate the vehicle away from massive half-buried boulders threatening to slash the underside away. Bumpy? It was completely treacherous. Because of the road conditions we parked in the lower parking area rather than driving on up to the trailhead at Kite Lake. The road had been empty, but making the turn into the parking lot, we were shocked that the lot was almost full. Cars lined the shoulders leading to the trailhead. There was even a line to the two port-a-potties near the information sign! What happened to our solitary wilderness hike?

To get our bearings we looked over the posted trail map, but it wasn't necessary. Looking to Mount Democrat, someone would have to be intoxicated or seriously demented to get lost. In the basin and above the tree line as far as the eye could see, people of all ages stretched out like ants on their way up the mountain. Some looked like hikers but many did not. One young person was even wearing flip flops.

It was a significant climb however, more difficult and much more crowded than I had imagined. Kathie was able to get three quarters of the way to the summit of Mount Democrat when she decided she was high enough and began the long descent. I made the summit and went on to reach the top of Mount Cameron, but my idea of climbing all four peaks of Route Combo had vanished.

Strangely, I found myself alone atop Mount Cameron, where I could see forever in any direction. I was filled with gratitude and thanked God for the moment - to be in good health in the midst of his creation. Just a few months before my world had been dark, but now it was bright and clear. I soaked up those moments of peace on the mountaintop because I knew how quickly life could change. I suspected my journey was not over and I would need God's peace and strength ahead.

Finally, it was time to go and found the trail to begin my descent. In the western sky, dark threatening clouds had gathered. The menacing threat disrupted the peace I felt and I quickened my step. It was time to get off the mountain and begin the long hike back.

One Buoy
at a Time

In previous chapters I have written of the many adventures and people who enriched my life and who I drew upon to navigate through my cancer journey. Ahead I describe my involvement with IRONMAN® triathlons for which, in part, I can thank Rick and Dick Hoyt from Boston, Massachusetts. They provided to me an example of faith, strength and resiliency under difficult odds.

When I thought about competing in an IRONMAN®, I believed it would be the ultimate test of endurance. It required dedication, courage and tremendous support from family and friends. But now, long after my last event, I'm facing a greater test of endurance. Still I draw upon those past experiences, and the example of people like the Hoyts, for strength and hope.

By late afternoon, I had settled into the sofa. My workout for the day was finished, household chores were done; it was a Saturday in December, and I was ready to relax. Feeling the softness of the cushions, I knew it wouldn't be long before I drifted into a welcomed nap.

But before I closed my eyes I turned on the television. It was set on Channel 11, the NBC affiliate. As the old 33 inch tube warmed up, I heard sports broadcaster Al Twautwig's voice as he described the action at the 2004 Ford IRONMAN® World Championship Triathlon in Kona, Hawaii.

I sat up and leaned forward. I had never seen an IRONMAN® triathlon before and had no interest in participating in one - but over the next two hours that would change. The dedication, courage and perseverance exhibited by the athletes made me believe anything was possible. It transcended anything I had previously seen in sport.

In 1978, John Collins, a Navy Commander, wanted to settle a debate as to who was the fittest of all endurance athletes; swimmers, cyclists or runners. To decide the argument, Collins created a race which combined three long distance events that already existed on the island of Oahu; the 2.4 mile Waikiki Roughwater Swim, the 112 mile Around Oahu Bike Race (originally a two day event), and the 26.2 mile Honolulu Marathon.

In 1981, the race moved to the Big Island to avoid Honolulu's traffic hazards. While the move from Waikiki's busy streets to Kona's barren lava fields made the race safer, it changed the nature of it. The IRONMAN® became a test not only of an athlete's endurance, but an epic battle against the Big Island's natural hazards. Along the Kona Coast, black lava rock dominates the panorama and against this backdrop, athletes cover the 140.6 miles battling long rolling hills, crosswinds, 95+ temperatures and scorching sun.

Today, the IRONMAN® triathlon has been described as the world's most challenging one-day endurance event. It still consists of a 2.4 mile swim, 112 mile bicycle ride and a 26.2 mile run, and is raced in that order and without a break. Most IRONMAN® events have a strict time limit of 17 hours to complete the race with separate cut off times for each discipline.

I listened intently as Trautwig gave this brief history of the IRONMAN®. He then explained how unforgiving and brutal the course was, describing the ocean swells and current in the Pacific, the fierce gusts which can literally blow a bike off the road, and the oppressive heat off the pavement.

My attention was really grabbed when NBC showed a clip of the 1997 IRONMAN® finish. Fighting exhaustion and extreme body cramps, competitors Sian Welch and Wendy Ingraham were unable to physically run or walk the last 300 feet to the finish and had to crawl on their hands and knees to the end. I moved to the edge of the sofa, transfixed by what I was seeing. The epic challenge of this race started working its way into me.

Next, NBC focused on several amateur athletes with amazing stories and who had overcome tremendous odds to be there. Two of those athletes were the father and son team of Rick and Dick Hoyt. They competed with a remarkable "can do it" attitude.

Rick Hoyt had been born with cerebral palsy. His doctors believed he would never be able to communicate and encouraged the Hoyts to institutionalize him. But his parents noticed Rick's eyes would follow them around the room. This gave them hope that somehow they would be able to connect. With persistence and dedication, the Hoyts taught Rick the alphabet. Then, when he was 11, they fitted him with a computer which tracked his eye movements to letters on the screen. This allowed him to speak. He began attending public schools and went on to graduate at the age of 21 from Boston University with a degree in Special Education.

"Team Hoyt" began in 1977 when Rick asked his father, Dick, if they could run a race together to benefit a fellow student who had become paralyzed. Even though Dick was not a runner, he agreed to his son's suggestion. After their first race Rick said, "Dad when I'm running, it feels like my disability disappears." Inspired by this, Dick began a regular running routine and "Team Hoyt" was born. The Hoyts went on to compete in numerous runs, marathons and seven IRONMAN® triathlons.

In the 2004 IRONMAN®, Dick used a harness to pull Rick in a rubber raft for the swim. For the bike section, Rick rode on the front of a specially designed bike. And Dick pushed Rick in his wheelchair for the run.

It was dark by the time Team Hoyt closed in on the finish in Kona. I could see in their faces that it had been a long day. As they approached the city's lights and the spotlights of the finish, tears welled up in my eyes. With grit and determination, Dick triumphantly pushed Rick past thousands of cheering spectators and across the finish line. It was an amazing display of human commitment and resounding proof that with faith and hard work you can accomplish anything.

The broadcast ended and I shut off the TV. I sat quietly for a long moment in my living room, slowly forming a new goal: I was going to be an IRONMAN®. Little did I know that in four years I would be racing in Kona in the World Championship and I would be there when Rick and Dick Hoyt were inducted into the IRONMAN® Hall of Fame. Equally unknown was that in six years I would get to meet them in person at a half-distance IRONMAN® race in New Hampshire.

With the vision of Rick and Dick Hoyt in my mind, I immediately started researching and planning. I quickly determined that, first, I would need a new bike, one meant specifically for triathlons;

my road bike simply wouldn't do. And, second, I'd need to experience a half-distance IRONMAN® triathlon. I purchased a TREK carbon OCLV triathlon bike with a three spoke HED rear wheel, registered for a half-distance IRONMAN® race in June - then registered for my first full-distance IRONMAN®, the Wisconsin IRONMAN® in September.

I began my training a few weeks later on a warm February day as I cycled 75 miles around Lake Pepin, a large body of water created by a widening of the Mississippi River. By March, after the Great Bear Chase cross country ski race in Michigan, I put away my skis and concentrated on running and cycling.

For the next 6 months, I worked at it. Not having a coach, I created my own training plan hoping to build endurance and strength in all three disciplines. On at least four days of the week, I alternated a swim at the local YMCA pool with a bike ride in the afternoon, or a bike ride followed by a run.

In May, after the ice cleared Potato Lake in front of our cabin, I began open water swimming. Given the cold water, a wet suit was a necessity. When swimming alone, I started to tie a five foot styrofoam noodle to my ankle with a two foot cord. My noodle (which was pink) offered little resistance and gave me something to float with if I needed it. It also helped identify my presence to motorboats.

Wisconsin's Potato Lake is not a mecca for triathlete swimmers; in fact, no one swims there. This is Green Bay Packer Country, home of hunters and beer drinking guys who love four-wheelers and snowmobiles. They fish and drive pontoons. So, a guy wearing a wetsuit, thermal cap, goggles and booties swimming with a pink noodle trailing behind made quite a sight. When my teenage daughter first saw her father approach the dock in this outfit, she turned to her mother and asked, "How come I couldn't have had a normal Dad?" Well, of course, you can't be normal doing this stuff; you have to be a little weird.

As part of my training, Kathie and I drove to Colorado where I biked and ran to prepare for the Leadville Marathon in July. This high altitude marathon was planned to build strength and oxygen capacity. My friend, Kevin Wentworth, arrived a few days later which gave him only one day to acclimate to the altitude.

On race day the two of us flat-landers lined up for the start on Main Street in Leadville (elevation 10,000 ft). We looked ahead to the course which began uphill for the first five miles. They fired the starting pistol and off we went. We ran in washed out gullies, on single track trails, across old mining roads and over large boulders, slowly climbing to the high point in the race at Mosquito Pass at elevation 13,185. It was an epic run with tremendous vistas and, for flat-landers, we finished respectably.

In September, after six months of training and several shorter practice events, I felt ready for my first IRONMAN® in Madison, Wisconsin. I wasn't ready, however, for the 95 degree heat or the oppressive humidity which greeted competitors that day.

We took off in the cool of the morning, and, despite the increasing temperature, most of the day went well. I had made it through the swim, finished the 112 miles of cycling and then, in the late evening, I had only the run to finish. When I made the turn for the second and final lap near the state capitol in the Wisconsin IRONMAN®, my legs were heavy and tired. The heat and humidity had worn me down. But I kept moving, heading toward State Street, the main bar/restaurant artery in Madison. Just ahead of me was an older runner beginning his first lap of the run. He had white hair, a large brace on one knee and tape on the other. He was hunched over, and hobbled with a slow and uneven gait. Dark framed glasses had been secured to his face with an athletic strap around the back of his head. He looked to be in significant discomfort, and, with a full marathon to go, I wondered how he was going to make it.

Even though I was crawling along, I passed him with an encouraging, "Way to go! Keep it going!" recognition. He said nothing but gave me a nod of acknowledgement.

Two years later at the 2007 Florida IRONMAN® Awards Banquet I would meet this individual and hear his story of hope, triumph and inspiration. His name was Frank Farrar and, years before at the age of 65, he was diagnosed with lymphoma. They told him he had two months to live. Farrar, a former one term governor of South Dakota, refused to accept the prognosis and began competing in IRONMAN® distance triathlons. Eventually, he went on to compete in at least 34 of them, and in 9 he qualified for the World Championships in Hawaii. Most importantly, Farrar's cancer went into remission. He told the Rapid City Journal in April of 2011, "I do it (IRONMAN® Triathlons) because it saved my life, and I'm a very strong advocate of exercise even though I'm not that good at it."

Despite the cancer remission and the amazing number of IRONMAN® events, the most inspiring aspect about Farrar was that he never quit. In an IRONMAN® triathlon, an athlete has 17 hours to complete the race. If they fail, they are considered a DNF (Did Not Finish). They are sent home with no medal and no results.

Seven times this happened to Farrar but it never kept him from going out to compete in another race. For this extraordinary man, it was all about getting to the start line and making the effort even in the face of challenges, setbacks and failures. He didn't quit at the prognosis of cancer and he wasn't going to quit because of a DNF.

Several years later when I was preparing for a speech, I called Frank at his home in Britton, South Dakota. The 85 year old athlete remarked that thanks to surgery, he now had a new back, a new eye, and a new knee. But even with all this new hardware, he told me he wanted to compete in one more IRONMAN®.

At the Madison triathlon, Farrar didn't make the time, but he wasn't alone. Because of the weather, the 2005 Wisconsin IRONMAN® had more dropouts than any previous IRONMAN® competition including those in Hawaii. I don't do well in hot conditions so I was thrilled to finish in fifth place in my age category with a time of 13 hours and 28 minutes.

My next IRONMAN® was Florida in 2007. I chose Florida primarily because it was a flat bike and run course and previous competitors described it as fast. I drove to Panama City with bike and gear stuffed in my car, arriving five days before the event to acclimate and review all three courses. Kathie flew down and joined me three days later.

I was nervous about the swim. This was my first sea swim in the Gulf of Mexico through deep water with the possibility of big waves, sharks, jellyfish, and other nasty stuff - and I'd be without my pink noodle. Gulp! My confidence had already been shaken by an experience a month earlier.

I had been in Biloxi, Mississippi doing church mission work after Hurricane Katrina. I thought it would be a great opportunity to season myself swimming in the Gulf of Mexico while I was there.

Once our church group arrived, I found a YMCA close to our temporary headquarters. Soon, I was practicing my swim stroke and getting comfortable with the pool water. Following my swim, I spoke to a middle-aged lifeguard who had been on duty and learned she was a swim instructor. After she voluntarily bestowed a few tips on my swim stroke, I told her I had signed up for the Florida IRONMAN® and asked her where I could practice a Gulf swim.

"Do you have a wetsuit?" she asked. "You'll need one to protect yourself from jelly fish."

"I do."

"Do you have swim booties? You'll need them to protect your feet from the stingrays which swim near the bottom of the bay."

"I do," I said.

"When will you be swimming?" she asked.

"Tomorrow afternoon."

"Okay," she said. "Watch out for sharks. They come out in late afternoon."

With that, I nervously began my exit, but she still wasn't done.

"Oh," she said, "and watch out for all the toxic debris from Hurricane Katrina!"

A month later I felt no more confident about swimming in the ocean, and I hoped the swim for the Florida triathlon would keep participants in relatively shallow waters. I figured it would start on the beach, go out a bit from shore, make a turn and head parallel to the coastline. Wrong! The course shot out in a straight line towards buoys so far out I couldn't see the last one out on the horizon. Fortunately, I had been practicing my visualization and positive coping thoughts to relax and prepare me for the Gulf swim.

On race day, I gathered with the other participants at the beach. With the rising sun, I could see the buoys stretched into the far distance. Ten minutes to the start I lined up with two thousand athletes on the beach. I dug my toes in the sand. Nervous, I did everything I could not to pee in my wet suit.

After the gun went off, this enormous mass of humanity crashed into the water, all of us jockeying for position. Arms and legs kicked up a plethora of splash, suds and spray. Swimmers were doing whatever they could to get out front. Any sharks or jellyfish in the water must have been traumatized by the pandemonium.

I had waited a few moments to allow the crush of swimmers to ease before I jumped in, but it didn't help. Soon I was in the washing-machine mix. Through the chaos, kicks and hits, I attempted to stay relaxed and focused on my coping thoughts. *Slow down*, I thought. *Focus on technique.* I repeated these phrases again and again. *Take one buoy at a time.*

I pushed further into deeper waters until the white sea floor suddenly dropped away into the blackness of deep abyss. My heart pounded. I kept lifting my head, trying to mark my direction as I swam out to some uncertain destination.

From the safety of the beach to the uncertainty of deep waters, life conditions change and present new challenges. I reminded myself that God was with me. I had used God's gift of imagination to mentally practice coping for this moment. I recalled my training and tried to stay positive with more thoughts like *I can do this* and *I am ready.*

After 2.4 miles I was happy to get out of the water and felt more confident as I climbed on my bike. With little wind and mild temperatures, my legs felt strong throughout the 112 miles and I knew I was in good placement. This was confirmed when I came out of the transition to the run and heard the announcer say I was in first place for my age category. I hung on through the run and finished with tears, joy and a huge sense of relief. Before I had fully cooled down, I committed myself to the 2008 World Championship.

At the awards banquet the next day I found out I had set a new course record in my age category. I also had the opportunity to meet Frank Farrar and began to learn his amazing story in overcoming cancer. Like Rick and Dick Hoyt, Farrar became an inspiration motivating me in my quest of the World Championship.

After the Florida IRONMAN®, my motivation to train was sky high. Since my training schedule was successful for the last two IRONMAN® events, I followed the same plan of two-a-day workouts while gradually increasing mileage in all three disciplines. By the end of May, I'd put over 1,700 miles on my bike, much of it cruising the 75 mile lap around Lake Pepin. Sometimes I would cycle the lap around Lake Pepin twice.

When the ice melted, I grabbed my pink noodle and swam in the lake outside our cabin and in the St. Croix River. On weekends, I'd typically head to open water and on weekdays do intervals (fast/slow 100's) in the local pool. Tuesday mornings I ran mile repeats at the high school track, Friday mornings I took a long ride on the bike and Sunday mornings I went for a long run. Thursdays I'd usually rest. While I had some semblance of order in the workout schedule, because of job and family responsibilities, flexibility was required in the plan.

My first preparatory competition was the Run for the Lakes Marathon in Brainerd, Minnesota. It took place in April, but a freak snowstorm hit on race day and by the ten mile mark I was running through six to eight inches of blowing snow. I could barely see the road for the rest of the race.

It was a far cry from the marathon I would do on the Big Island where I was worried about the heat. I had heard it helped to train in sweat clothes (as long as you consume an adequate amount of water), so by mid-August I was wearing sweat pants and sweatshirt in my workouts. I went out looking like the Pillsbury Doughboy.

One warm August morning, I bundled up and set out with Chuck Balzer for the cabin some 140 miles away. Chuck was happily dressed in his customary attire of bike shorts and a short sleeve bike jersey. As the doughboy, I started sweating just pumping air in the tires.

We rode 80 miles on back roads from Red Wing through Wisconsin to the little town of Ridgeland. Although there was little wind, my sweat-soaked doughboy attire weighed a ton and was as aerodynamic as a Mac Truck. Chuck, however, seemed to enjoy drafting behind me.

A little past the halfway mark, Chuck turned on a desolate road which would eventually take him back to Red Wing. Now alone, I continued north until I came upon two cyclists decked out in their cycling shorts, team jerseys and dark glasses. This perspiring doughboy pulled alongside of them and asked where Highway M connected. One of the cyclists asked where I was from. When I told them, I got a silent stunned response.

Yes, you gotta be a little weird doing this stuff! I took it in stride and pedaled on to the cabin. By the way, the sweat clothes scheme didn't make a difference. The heat in Hawaii was still brutal.

Finally, it was the morning of the Hawaii IRONMAN®. My body was marked, tires pumped up, sunscreen on, and, after ten minutes of struggle, I had successfully squeezed into my non-floatation swim skin suit. After an anxious wait with Kathie and Keri near the King Kamehameha Hotel, it was time to go. We said goodbye with hugs and words of encouragement. Then I made my way into the transition area with hundreds of other athletes.

The predawn darkness had given way to the Kona sunrise which I barely noticed in the surrounding chaos. Thirty minutes to the start! My heart pounded but I continued to follow other athletes down the narrow steps leading to the water and swim start.

I felt uncertain. It had been a long journey to get there. Even with four years of training, countless miles on the bike and run, and two previous IRONMAN® competitions, finishing this race was still a gamble. The swim, a single lap 2.4 non-wet suit ocean swim, had been described by Active.com, as "one of the toughest in the sport." The ever present swells wreck havoc with a swim stroke and the tidal current pulls swimmers out which leads to a fast first half but a grueling second. The bike course on the Big Island is full of long rolling hills set in the extreme heat of endless, lonely black lava fields. The severe winds on the island are legendary and vary in intensity from steady to heavy blasts that can blow a rider across the road.

Several days before the race Kathie and I drove with our son, Erik, to the turnaround point of the bike course approximately 50 miles from Kona. Seeing the barren and exposed western coastline of the Big Island, it finally sunk in how hard this race was going to be. Erik attempted to reassure me, but added, "Dad, that's why they call it the IRONMAN®!"

Finishing the bike portion can be a bittersweet victory as it begins the marathon run in the afternoon heat. Runners wind around Kona on Alii Drive, then climb up Palani Street to the Queen Ka'ahumanu Highway to make their way out to the Natural Energy Lab. The Official Qualifying Guide states, "Unless cloud cover or nightfall spares you, anticipate high heat and humidity."

This is what I was facing as the clock ticked away to the start. With fifteen minutes to go, two Navy Seal sailors dropped from an aircraft into the water. The thousands lining the waterfront cheered loudly. Native Hawaiians on the seawall pounded out a rhythm on drums. An NBC helicopter hovered above us. With all this noise, it was difficult to make out the announcer's instructions.

Ten minutes to the start I moved down the steps to the small beach where hundreds of athletes stood or treaded water near the start. All were serious and there was little talk. I adjusted my swim cap and goggles and assessed my starting position. Swimmers moved to the line as I strained to see beyond the first buoy. Without my glasses it was impossible. I fought back fears by reviewing what I had practiced over and over. *Take one buoy at a time*, I repeated. *Relax and enjoy this part of the race*. I waded into the water about halfway between the start line and the beach. Soon I was treading water. I could feel the swells and observed a slight chop in the water.

A few minutes before the start an almost mystical sense of calm engulfed me. After years of anticipation, seven months of training and weeks of planning, the race was finally here. I had done my homework and earned a spot in one of the most highly competitive events anywhere in the world. Finish or bail, I was grateful to be there. I was grateful for my family and friends who had come to support and encourage me. I took a moment and thanked God to be healthy enough to even consider undertaking the event.

The start corral became more congested and I lost all sense of time. I set my stopwatch anticipating the start was minutes away, but then the cannon fired and it was time to allow my prepared body and mind to take over. My head went down, my legs came up and I was off. Soon I was enveloped in a liquid medium. Mayhem swirled around me with limbs thrashing and kicking.

I repeated my mantra to relax, focus on my stroke and reminded myself to take one buoy at a time. The clear water, except for millions of tiny bubbles churned up from the hundreds of swimmers, allowed a view of the silent sea floor below. Every three to four strokes I looked up trying to spot the first buoy but all I could see were arms, legs and spray.

Several times a swimmer would strike my legs and someone's hand once came crashing down on my head. But my goggles stayed on and body parts remained intact, so I kept pushing farther out into the bay.

Spotting a buoy required a sense of timing. Often, I'd look up at the bottom of a swell and see nothing but water and flailing arms. Still, I passed one buoy, then another and another.

Finally, I reached the turnaround point a mile out from the pier: a sailboat moored in 90 feet of water. Circling it, I was exposed to a significant chop in the sea swells. At this point, the swimmers were forced to converge and, like an eight lane highway at rush hour reducing to two lanes, swimmers fought for position.

I looked to spot Kona and the finish but again it was all water, legs and arms. And again, I had to remind myself to take it one buoy at a time. In this way, I eventually reached the beach. My arms were exhausted and in a semi-stupor of fatigue, I concentrated on looking somewhat coherent climbing the steps to the showers and transition area, knowing that thousands of cheering people were watching on the seawall.

I hurried though the showers with gear bag in hand, then scrambled to change in the dressing tent for the next leg. For me, the swim was the scariest section and I was relieved to have finished. Now I was on my bike and it felt like the race had truly begun.

Out of the transition we started down Kuakini Highway and I was immediately humbled by the large number of bikers who were long ahead of me. I followed the road to a turnaround which led to the Queen Ka'ahumanu Highway. As I pedaled I reminded myself this was my strength; this was where I needed to make up time.

As we rode out of Kailua-Kona, the cheering crowds gave way to the hot silence of the lava fields stretching for miles in every direction. There were few trees or vegetation to block the sun or the wind. From that point on, there would be no place to hide; it was just me and the road.

The sun bore down from an almost cloudless sky, but my legs felt strong and I passed many riders. I was making good time, moving between 20 to 24 mph. On the long downhills my speed reached over 30 mph and I felt great. Around the 30 mile mark, however, I realized why things had been going so well. The movement of a few small bushes at roadside revealed a significant tailwind. Helpful now, but there would be hell to pay on the return.

Close to the town of Kawaihae the wind mysteriously shifted and a strong side wind slammed against the long procession of bikers. The heat off the asphalt intensified and the sun baked my head in its helmet. Riders in the distant horizon appeared blurry as in a desert mirage. I hydrated frequently and resupplied water at every aid station. I also began popping electrolyte replacement pills and GU packets to keep my body refueled.

From the village of Kawaihae, the road began a long climb to the turnaround point at Hawi. I attempted to keep my arms on the aero bars, but the sudden gusts of wind forced me to stabilize the bike with hands on the handlebars. My pace slowed dramatically as the climb and winds took their toll. My back ached and the steady howl of wind in my ears wore at me. Because of the conditions, I decided to wait until after the turnaround to eat my sandwich and cherry pie.

At the base of the long climb I first heard the helicopter on its return to Kona. Immediately thereafter the lead motorcycle came into view with the first place athlete not far behind. Then the riders began to pass; first it was a trickle but soon a steady stream of cyclists flew down the long hill.

I passed three competitors on the side of the road with flats or other mechanical problems, and my mind shifted from the status of my legs to the status of my bike. I knew a hundred things could go wrong but I tried to think positively.

At the turnaround I consumed the food stuffed in my back pocket and started the long downhill. As my speed increased, wind pounding my left side became more forceful and unpredictable. As a result, I was again frequently forced out of the aero bars to stabilize the bike.

We turned south on the Queen K Highway and my fears that there would be hell to pay on the return were confirmed. With 40 miles to go, the headwind became brutal and I was no longer passing riders. Everyone around me labored silently and no one looked happy. The lava fields reappeared and, with each mile, I longed for my arrival into Kona. This was not a good sign as with each hill overtaken I faced yet another long hill to climb.

Finally, the city limits came into sight and I began to mentally review the bike/run transition. I coasted into the area then hurried into the dressing tent where a volunteer was there to assist me.

Having a personal attendant was helpful, but he kept trying to speed up the transition process. He grabbed at my jersey when I just wanted to sit, even just for a few minutes, or perhaps a few hours, or maybe for the rest of the day. The next four or five hours looked bleak. It was 2:30pm on a hot afternoon and 26.2 miles stretched ahead of me. But I allowed the volunteer to keep me moving. I wasn't quick, but I didn't stop. Like so many times in life when we feel like we have nothing left, when the task ahead seems to be impossibly overwhelming, there is only one thing to do; keep getting up and, no matter how slowly, keep moving forward.

Fortunately, my training for this race had focused primarily on the run. To ensure that I'd have enough strength left, I accumulated more running miles and more brick sessions (bike, then immediately run) for this than the other two IRONMAN® events. But as I ran out of the transition area, I quickly discovered that everything hurt. The heat, hills and wind had taken their toll on my legs and

the prospect of running 26.2 miles was daunting.

The run course began up Palani Road to Alii Drive where at mile three I saw Kathie and the kids. My hope was that in those first few miles my legs would adjust, but by the time I saw them (a wonderful sight) I was still hurting and had serious doubts if I could make it to the finish. Kathie realized things were not going well and offered a drink of water, but I had to refuse as the rules state no runner can be assisted by family or spectators.

My immediate goal was just get to the next aid station. Once there, I found refuge and time to set a strategy in a warm port-a-potty where I was able to temporarily close myself off from the racers and crowds. I slowed my thinking and made a plan. Rather than focus on the 23 miles I had left, I decided to set small goals of running one mile to the next aid station where I'd reward myself with sponges, water, ice and orange slices. Then I'd focus only on the next mile, reward myself, then focus on the next. Each aid station became an oasis in a hot, stifling desert. By the time I saw my family again at mile eight my outlook had improved, although the periodic tightening in my hamstring hadn't helped my pace.

Off Alii Drive, the course brought runners onto the Queen K Highway then out to the Natural Energy Lab and the turnaround. The sun setting over the Pacific was beautiful, but, with six miles to go, it became clear that my goal of finishing in daylight had been dashed. I was depleted and the aid stations couldn't come soon enough.

Those who have run a marathon know the last six miles are really another race. You're closer to the finish but that final stretch becomes a separate monumental challenge to overcome. As my legs thudded against the pavement, my mind retraced the day. So much had happened already and the race had lost its luster; I just wanted to be done. I just wanted to be home. In the next few miles however, I was about to encounter two defining situations which transformed this adventure into a treasured experience.

By mile 20 I was running alone in almost total darkness. Whatever light there may have been in this rural area was immediately absorbed by the lava fields and for a long time I was only able to see two to three feet in front of me. Then I squinted ahead and spotted what appeared to be a small light coming towards me. My eyes were tired and without glasses I couldn't make it out. Was it an LED light? Confusingly, it was low to the ground. I wondered if it was a runner with a light on her/his leg, except it lacked an up and down movement.

After another minute, the light grew close enough to make out. Through the darkness I realized it was an athlete with no legs in a low-to-the-ground hand cycle pedaling his way out to the Energy Lab. It dawned on me as I watched him pass. He swam the same 2.4 miles in the Pacific Ocean swells; he biked the same 112 miles against the same unrelenting wind; and now, with only his arms, he was facing the same run.

The race made sense again. It wasn't about time. It wasn't about who won or who received the awards. It wasn't even about finishing. No, it was about faith. The IRONMAN® was about making the effort, getting out of comfort zones and putting oneself in an arena where both success and failure were possibilities. It was about taking the risk, and facing the unknowns and the mental barriers that hold us back. It was about the hand cyclist and others in life who, despite the crosses they carried, were out there exhausted and uncertain and yet dare to keep pushing themselves forward.

This understanding energized me through the last couple of miles until I began seeing the lights of Kona. Coming up a long hill, I approached a quiet but well lit intersection where the Queen K divided into various Kona streets. I was about to experience my second treasured moment.

Three miles from the finish, I came through the intersection. Off to my right was a small group of spectators. Suddenly, I saw Dave Roseen, my friend, colleague and running mentor. This was the man who some 25 years earlier had suggested that I, a non-athlete, join him in a relay triathlon. I wouldn't have been there without his example and encouragement to be active.

Our eyes met. I waved and yelled, but Dave didn't say anything. He didn't come out on the road but started running with me on the sidewalk, darting in and out of more and more people lining the streets. Sometimes I wouldn't see him and then he would reappear, running in silence nearby. He wasn't there to cheerlead or offer advice. He was there as he has been throughout our friendship providing the example, the positive strength and reassurance to believe in myself.

As I turned on Alii Drive and reached the hundreds of cheering people lining the street, Dave disappeared into the crowd. Without fanfare or without recognition, he was gone. When I looked up, the finish was in sight.

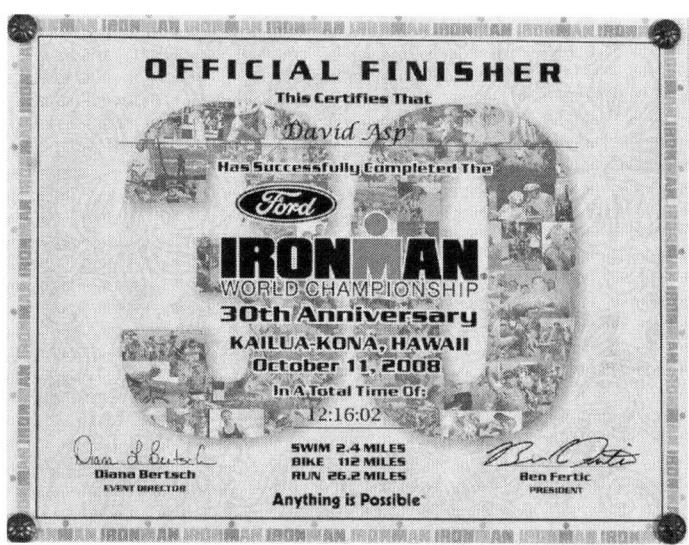

Triumph
over
Tragedy

F eeling high from the hike up Route Combo, I was looking forward to fall and the ski season. My cancer was in remission and I was feeling increasingly hopeful. Although cancer, even in retreat, continues to cast long shadows. If a small ache develops, nagging questions arise like, "Is my cancer back?" or "Has it grown?" Before my diagnosis, I assumed that a strange pain would simply clear up on its own, and it usually did. After I started my cancer journey, however, even the smallest twinge would result in apprehension and often a call to the medical team for answers.

I've learned that humans have a voracious desire to have their questions answered. From these small aches to more significant questions like, "Why me?" and "Where is God when we suffer?" we seek understanding. We live in world that is imperfect, however; a world where bad things happen. And as soon as we think we understand one problem, another one arises.

For me, when the answers are elusive and the road ahead is uncertain, it has been critical to call upon my faith in God. Like a coach, my faith in God helps me reframe the situation when bad things happen. Effective coaches teach their athletes to use adversity to increase their confidence rather than erode it. They help athletes use adversity to work for them rather than against them, to find the advantage in a disadvantage.

Rabbi Harold Kushner, in his book Why Do Bad Things Happen to Good People, puts it this way. "The God I believe in does not send us the problem. He gives us the strength to cope with the problem. I believe that God gives us the strength and patience and hope, renewing our spiritual resources when they run dry" (Kushner 1981).

Kushner goes on to describe human beings as 'God's language.' God expresses his love for us by sending friends and neighbors to relieve and ease our burdens. The Lord is present when people help others in need.

God demonstrates His love and compassion in various ways - from the very creation of this world to people helping others who are hurting. God is there in the medical researchers, doctors, nurses and technicians who devote their lives to finding cures and helping the sick. In my cancer journey, the Lord sent angels in the form of friends and neighbors, who prayed, sent cards and brought meals to ease the burden.

As my cancer journey progressed from a 5K run all the way to a marathon with an uncertain finish, it has become important to understand how other people have coped with life crises. I wanted to know the characteristics and beliefs of people who didn't allow adversity to dominate their lives. How did they preserve their health, marriage and sanity in the face of tragedy?

Anyone who has life goals cannot avoid setbacks that invariably occur along the journey. And when we love someone, we run the risk of losing that person to separation and/or death. While most of us cope relatively well, tragedies can negatively impact lives. A life threatening illness, childhood abuse or the anguish of a loss can impact one's health, marriage and happiness.

Having spent the last forty years as a psychologist, I have had the honor to hear stories of ordinary people coping in the face of horrific challenges. When I started, I didn't realize the impact these stories would have on me. I didn't know, as I tried to help them, how much they were helping me. To be invited to be a part of people's vulnerabilities, to share in testimonies of truths and hear stories of resilience, has been a cherished gift.

Throughout my career, I've worked with people on both ends

of the spectrum. There were those who coped extremely well and moved forward after a crisis. There were others, however, who became consumed by the adversity and got stuck in anger, fear or resentment. It was as if they became frozen in an ever-present effort to seek answers or receive retribution.

Life's journey need not be filled with anger, bitterness, fear or depression. Rather the journey can be one of purpose, courage, faith and dignity. We may not control life's circumstances, but we do have control over what we believe and what we do with those circumstances.

Following, are two stories of extraordinary people turning heartbreaking setbacks into comebacks and ultimately experiencing triumph through tragedy.

When a person of color entered my therapy practice, I took special note. Even though their struggles may be similar to a white person, people of color will experience oppression and racial bias.

One such person was a middle age woman who came to my office struggling in a co-dependent relationship and experiencing depression. She had come to our small town by way of the local women's shelter and was attempting to live independently in a predominately white community.

"Grace" grew up in a nearby city as the oldest of three girls and two brothers. Her father was nonexistent and her mother was an alcoholic which created a chaotic and uncertain childhood. As a result, Grace spent the majority of her childhood raised by her aunt. By age 17 she was pregnant and dropped out of high school.

Working various jobs to make ends meet, Grace was introduced to cocaine in her early 20s and became addicted. A short stay in a treatment program temporarily interrupted her drug use, but she relapsed after becoming pregnant again.

Grace's life continued to fall apart and she plunged deeper into despair. She went on welfare and lost custody of her children. She lost her home and started living on the streets.

As a child she had grown up in a church community thanks to

her aunt's influence. Homeless and despairing, she longed for her church community and the warmth and comfort it could provide. Unfortunately, even though she retained her faith, she was too embarrassed to return to her church.

She moved into a shelter and received help. She was then able to enter another treatment program and live in a co-op. For a while, things started looking up. Grace found employment and fought to get her kids back. She did what she could to fight off drugs and stay off the street - but the chains of addiction were strong.

Soon, Grace began another downward spiral, this time into a gambling addiction. For more than a year she struggled with terrible debt. The bank had to repossessed her car and her aunt needed to bail her out financially.

Finally, Grace checked herself into an 18 month inpatient treatment program, and this time she didn't cut corners. She did the hard work and accepted the assistance given.

In treatment, she connected with a sponsor and maintained contact with her aunt. Grace's sponsor provided unconditional acceptance and her aunt was a constant rock of support. Grace told me, "I could tell my aunt anything and we would talk for hours." Her aunt never gave up sticking with her through the narrow, difficult parts of her journey. She demonstrated the grace of God, forgiving and loving Grace unconditionally on her return home.

When Grace walked in my office she was free from drugs. She was making a new life for herself and had enrolled in an online divinity school. Through faith in God and the help of others, she found strength to do more than she ever believed she was capable of doing. With quiet heroism, she picked up the pieces of her life and began to live again.

Eventually the love of God came full circle as Grace returned to the city to care for her elderly aunt. The two together demonstrated God's language by helping each other through their journeys.

Grace's comeback was a story of faith, triumph and coming home.

We believe the natural process of life is that we precede our children in death. As parents, we're conditioned to care and protect our children from infancy to adulthood. We imagine growing older with our children having children, experiencing family vacations and holidays with our grandchildren. For the Goetz family, those constructs were shattered. It's hard to imagine any greater loss than losing a child. The Goetz family experienced the unthinkable tragedy of losing two children.

I've been blessed to have had a friendship with Bob and Susan Goetz and their daughter Stephanie. Somehow these three survived and have thrived despite their devastating losses. Through the years I have seen them flourish and now needing to know how, I interviewed them to find answers.

On a beautiful Friday afternoon in October of 1997, Bob and Susan's oldest son Brandon was hit by a truck and killed attempting to cross the main thoroughfare through Red Wing. Brandon was returning from delivering medications to patients as part of his job at Corner Drug where his father was a lead pharmacist. At 17, Brandon, a senior, had his life ahead of him. He was a responsible teenager, a good student and an accomplished tennis player.

Bob and Susan grew up in western North Dakota in a Christian faith tradition. They had lived in the bluffs of the Mississippi River in Red Wing for 16 years. Susan was a teacher and Bob a pharmacist, and they were well known and respected in the small community.

Bob and Susan had two other children. Cameron was fifteen and out of town at a cross country meet on that fateful Friday. Stephanie was thirteen and getting ready for an early Halloween party.

At the hospital, Bob and Susan attempted to grasp their enormous loss as the news of Brandon's death spread. Within hours the hospital began to fill with friends and students coming to express their shock and grief. School officials cancelled the football game and organized an assembly the next day to help students, friends and family process and receive support.

As most people do, the Goetz's struggled with the question of why. Their religious beliefs had told them that God was in control of their lives, but now that belief seemed to no longer make sense. Still, they fought the inclination to doubt and be angry. The foundation of their deep spiritual philosophy was to trust God above all else. Susan said, "We may not understand how God works, but ultimately we know God is good."

The outpouring of support and love received from the community softened their loss. For Bob and Susan, the compassion of others represented God's response and reaffirmed their connection with Him. Instead of being stuck in grief, the Goetz's spiritual connection became a mission to help others know the God they trusted.

Because of Brandon's love of Christian music, Bob began organizing Christian music concerts of nationally recognized artists for the community. Many of Brandon's friends stayed connected and as a result, Bob and Susan opened their home for a weekly Bible study. The tremendous support helped Bob and Susan move forward.

For Cameron and Stephanie, the loss of their brother was difficult to grasp. Despite their grief, both kids excelled in academics and athletics, and by 2001 Cameron had graduated and began his first semester at the University of Wisconsin-Green Bay on a tennis scholarship. From the outside, all signs indicated Cam was doing well with his new life in college, but on the inside, something was amiss. A fog of despair had crept in that seemed to make the smallest tasks into monumental chores.

It was hard to know when the sun had stopped shining and the inner darkness began, but Cameron knew something wasn't right and courageously sought help through medication and therapy. Bob and Susan did what they could to penetrate his dark moods, but depression can choke back the need to express feelings.

After completing his first year of college, Cam came home to work as a waiter at the St. James Hotel. He spent the summer working, reconnecting with friends and playing tennis. On the surface it appeared nothing was wrong, but the episodes of despondency persisted until, on a Sunday afternoon in August, the pain became too much.

After attending church, Bob, Susan, Stephanie and Bob's mother drove to Minneapolis to visit a family member who was terminally ill. Cameron stayed home to work. That afternoon Cam's best friend Adam was flying home to Red Wing when he suddenly began sobbing as he listened to the newly released song by Mercy Me, "I Can Only Imagine." He couldn't understand why. Around the same time, Cam's friend CJ rang the doorbell. He had come by the house to play tennis and when no one answered, he knocked. Getting no response, CJ assumed Cameron was not at home and left.

Some time later, Bob dropped Susan at the house before returning his mother to her home. Susan entered the kitchen and immediately noticed an eerie silence. A few minutes later she found Cam. A day before his 20th birthday, and almost five years from his brother's death, Cameron had ended his life by suicide.

It is particularly difficult for survivors to cope with a suicide death. They can experience confusion, anger and a feeling of betrayal by the departed. Survivors may harbor feelings of guilt or self-doubt for not recognizing the signs. In addition, there may be a stigma of shame in the aftermath.

Like most survivors of a suicide death, Bob and Susan sought to understand how and what led their beautiful son to this decision. They agonized about the unreasonable guilt they placed on themselves. Susan stated, "Suicide is so convoluted. Your parenting task is to care for your children. With suicide there's this huge guilt of not being able to save the person you love."

As parents, they felt the anguish and hurt knowing the enormous pain their son had felt. And they carried the hurt as well for Stephanie and their aged parents who were also dealing with the loss. They again struggled with questions of God, "What is going on?" and "Why are we asked to walk this walk twice."

A second time around it would have been easy to give in to the doubts and lose faith in God. But Susan told me, "I needed to make a paradigm shift in my interpretation of what God has said." She wasn't questioning what God said, but reinterpreting her understanding of God's word. Susan and Bob knew God was not the author of death but the One who gives glory to life. Together, they chose the courageous path to not give up, but to trust God's bigger plan.

Aware that adversity can tear lives apart, Bob and Susan made a commitment to each other. They promised to talk about the loss, and share their pain and faith together. Beyond their own grief, they were also aware of the love and support Stephanie needed from them to cope.

Vulnerability is a sign of strength. Bob and Susan were open about their faith and sharing their grief. They opened themselves to receive help and found a community that responded with incredible support. It was part of what they learned growing up in a Christian tradition in North Dakota. "You operate in life that you don't shrink from a challenge. You believe in yourself and continue to develop your spiritual intelligence."

Six months after Cameron died, Susan developed a Grief Share support group in conjunction with a colleague who also experienced a recent loss. Bob and Susan researched facts about depression and suicide. They began helping others who had experienced a suicide loss. They raised money and provided educational awareness through community forums. To Bob and Susan, it was the Holy Spirit speaking from within. They believed Christ's life exemplified helping others, serving rather than being served. As a bedrock of their Christian philosophy, it was the only choice that made sense.

For Bob, it became about recognizing what he now had. Bob said, "I looked at what was lost and then what I had left. Now it's about, what am I going to do with what I have left?"

A couple who walked away from doubt and negativity bravely chose to see life in a different way. They chose to save their marriage and strengthen the potential for a rewarding life. They were ordinary people demonstrating an extraordinary resilience.

After Brandon's death, Stephanie felt closer to her brother Cameron. "He and I were the only things left." However, when Cam died, Stephanie said, "I lost both of my protectors, my big brothers." Her double grief erased many of the childhood memories she had with them and for years she grieved in relative silence.

Years later she became a news anchor for a major television station in Fargo, North Dakota. There, the traumatic stories of car accidents, murder and suicide triggered deeply hidden emotions. Along with the immeasurable sadness came fear and anxiety. "Am I like my brother?" she'd worry. "If depression happened in my family, can it happen to me?"

Being a prominent figure in the community, it took courage for Stephanie to seek professional help. Through therapy, Stephanie began to express her feelings and unearth the buried emotions. She learned ways to deal with stress and anxiety including meditation. In the process, she became educated about depression and mental illness which decreased her fears.

Slowly, she put one foot in front of the other and raised herself out of her black hole. Stephanie learned that life can be beautiful again. She mastered skills so when crises would occur, she could weather the storms. For her, death created a larger capacity to love and a more urgent need for it, knowing how quickly it can be gone. Stephanie said, "Little petty things don't matter; it's making sure to have the quality times with friends and family." She also learned the importance of giving herself time to feel uncomfortable and grieve. Lastly, she realized when there is help available, no one should go through the despair of depression and anxiety.

Stephanie had a dream to use her new awareness to help others struggling with mental illness. Her dream became a "can do it" project to develop a mental illness/wellness nonprofit initiative to connect kids in elementary, middle and high school to mental health care. She worked with local medical associations, school administrators and a psychiatrist who had developed a similar program in St. Cloud, Minnesota. Stephanie's vision turned into a reality when a close friend and several other passionate advocates joined the effort to establish the non-profit Stephanie Goetz Foundation.

Monies raised through the Foundation provided local school districts with mental health facilitators helping hundreds of students and parents with counseling and assessments. Thousands of others were helped through the ripple effect when mental health information was shared and stigmas erased. The Foundation, now called the Goetz Mental Wellness Initiative and Imagine Thriving, has touched thousands of lives by connecting struggling youth with the mental health resources they need, by educating communities on how to be healthy, and by bringing hope and healing to those struggling with mental illness.

A young woman turned a tragedy into a cause and made a choice to save her life. In the process, she benefitted the lives of hundreds, possibly thousands, of others.

The Goetz family demonstrated remarkable resiliency. Having survived two devastating losses, they were called upon to do more than they ever believed they were capable of doing.

Grace and the Goetz family come from very different places, but in their own ways, they each found the strength not to give up on God. They got themselves back to the start line, turned personal tragedy into quiet heroism, and helped others in the process.

Alcatraz

This 2010 adventure challenged my physical and psychological limits. The water in San Francisco Bay was cold, the current was strong and Alcatraz Island looked as sinister as one could imagine. The night before the event, I was convinced I had made a mistake.

I have this quote from President Theodore Roosevelt's 1910 speech on a plaque in my office:

"It's not the critic who counts; not the man who points how the strong man stumbles, or where the doer of deeds could have done them better. The credit belongs to the man who is actually in the arena, whose face is marred by dust and sweat and blood; who strives valiantly; who errs, who comes up short again and again, because there is no effort without error and shortcoming, but who does actually strive to do the deeds; who knows the great enthusiasms, the great devotions; who spends himself in a worthy cause; who at best knows in the end the triumph of high achievement, and who at the worst, if he fails, at least he fails while daring greatly, so that his place shall never be with those cold and timid souls who know neither victory or defeat."

I decided to swim the 1.4 miles from Alcatraz to the mainland in San Francisco Bay as a way to challenge vulnerabilities. Even after years of IRONMAN® training, I still had a fear of open water swimming and I needed to put myself back in the arena.

Years before, when I first had the desire to compete in a full triathlon, I had become an accomplished cyclist and runner but didn't know how to swim. I never had lessons and what I thought was swimming (head out of the water) was a far cry from real swimming. Fortunately, our local YMCA had a program led by a former high school coach which taught freestyle swimming, the most common stroke in a triathlon. He worked with a group of us at the pool on Saturday mornings to improve our technique and strength in the water.

The pool was comfortable, the group was fun, and I learned a great deal. After a few months, I believed I was ready for my first full triathlon, the Tinman in Menomonie, Wisconsin. The race was a half IRONMAN®, making the swim about 1.2 miles. Unknown to me at the time, Lake Menomonie was filled with green algae. It was so bad that several years later the race was cancelled because of pollution dangers.

I quickly discovered swimming in open water was significantly different than swimming in a pool. In open water you can encounter wind, sun, waves, seaweed, currents, even sharks and jellyfish if you're in the ocean. In open water, there is no line to guide you, no comforting wall to grab, and usually no bottom to see.

Additionally, racing presents its own challenges. Forward progress is often impeded by the currents and waves. The course is usually marked by small buoys which can be difficult to see from water level. This requires more heads-up swimming which alters one's stroke cycle and causes the legs to drop deeper in the water which slows one's speed. And in the mass start of most races it's common to get bumped or hit by other swimmers.

I knew none of this as I stepped into Lake Menomonie for my first triathlon.

As the race director instructed swimmers into the water for the start, I attempted to find a place in swallow water void of weeds. Unable to see the bottom I could only feel a rough, sedgy and weedy place to stand on. The gun went off and I took a few steps into deeper water. Then, with both arms extended, I dove into a soup bowl of murky, dense algae! Yikes!

My heart rate climbed as I swam through pea soup. There was no clarity, no sense of direction, just an uncharted, mysterious peril. With no sense of appropriate pacing or depth, my heart rate continued to rise. A minute out from the start I looked to the first buoy and thought, *That's a long way.* My head fell back into the pea soup. A few strokes later I pulled my head up to again assess progress. To my distress, the buoy didn't look any closer. This triggered my next thought, *I'm not going to make it.*

There was no pool wall to grab, no boats or race assistants to help me. I was quite literally in over my head. I began panicking as I struggled to tread water. Finally, it dawned on me to just float. I could always just float. Soon I began to calm down and started swimming again. I figured if I could make it to the nearest buoy, I could hold on, get my bearings and get help.

When I got there, I held on and it gave me some sense of stability and relief. There were no boats in view but with this small accomplishment I decided to go for the next buoy. When I made it there I knew I had enough strength to make it to the next. This was my first triathlon swim experience: one buoy to the next while I struggled to keep from panicking. It wasn't pretty, but I got through it.

This initial trauma rattled my confidence and created a conditioned fear which reappeared at every future open-water swim, including the three IRONMAN® events. Like all experiences, however, even traumatic ones, I learned a great deal. I was determined that from then on, I would prepare myself both physically and mentally for what I would likely face.

I learned to assess the swim course, pace myself, and know the temperature and quality of the water. I practiced open water swims in the St. Croix and Mississippi Rivers and in the lake in front of our Wisconsin cabin. I practiced a mental visualization meditation to lessen doubt, bolster confidence, and help me anticipate the race in a positive manner.

In spite of all of it, I was never able to completely eliminate the fears that competitive open swims caused me. I continued however, to face those fears. Since that first swim in Lake Menomonie, I've swam Sprint, Olympic, half and full IRONMAN® distances. I've swam in clear water and murky water. I've swam in rivers, canals, lakes, and oceans. I've swam in both warm and cold weather. I've swam in calm water, rough water, in rain storms and brilliant sunshine. I've swam in waters lurking with jellyfish, stingrays, sharks and alligators. I did it because I enjoyed the challenge, but also because I wanted to push myself to the limit.

Then I heard about Alcatraz, a 1.4 mile swim from the old prison across San Francisco Bay to Aquatic Park on the mainland. It promised water temperatures of 55 degrees and fierce currents. Most organized Alcatraz swims (Alcatraz Crossing, Alcatraz Sharkfest, Alcatraz Challenge and Escape From Alcatraz) demand that swimmers are strong and familiar with tides and currents. Knowledge of the current is critical and you have to account for it as you set the direction of your swim. If you set out from Alcatraz aiming directly at Aquatic Park for instance, the current will sweep you west out into the shipping canal, under the Golden Gate Bridge and eventually out into the Pacific Ocean. Not a good result! Knowing all this, it was a swim I had to do.

I was signed up for the Big Sur Marathon and with it I would be attending my wife's family reunion in April of 2010. This offered a perfect opportunity to make the swim. Fortunately, I heard of an individual who had a business coaching swimmers to accomplish the Alcatraz swim. For a fee, he'd supply a boat, a captain and critical information. The plan was to complete the swim Saturday and then drive to Monterey to pick up my marathon race packet for the run the next day.

I arrived on Friday and checked in with my coach on the phone. He encouraged me to go for a swim at Aquatic Park in order to get accustomed to the bitterly cold water. After checking in to our motel, Kathie and I went to the waterfront with wet suit in hand. We were anxious to see the area and after the practice swim, we planned to close out the evening with a romantic dinner in Fisherman's Wharf.

Temperatures by late afternoon were cool with dark overcast skies. As we approached the bay, flags at the Park stood straight out and snapped from the force of the gusts. The bay itself was engulfed in large white-capped waves. The rough, angry water was dark gray, almost black, and Alcatraz looked foreboding and impossibly far away. In a moment, my excitement for a glorious adventure turned into threatening dread.

I dipped my hand in the water and the cold stung my fingers. That was it; I became too overcome with worry to even put my wet suit on, let alone go for a swim.

I struggled through our dinner at a nice Italian restaurant. I began thinking I was crazy for coming up with this idea, that it was too much and I had gone over the top. Not wanting to ruin her evening, I kept my fears from Kathie, but in my mind I was furiously running through ideas on how to honorably get out of my predicament.

It was a sleepless night at the motel. Hoping hot water would help, I sat in the bathtub around 2:00 a.m. and tried to think pleasant, reassuring thoughts. Unfortunately, I kept hearing the roaring wind outside and remembered the white-capped, angry bay. At 6:00 a.m. I received a surprise call from Rick Mollgaard asking if I wanted to ride with him later in the morning. He had forgotten I was on the West Coast but it was good diversion to hear his voice.

My swim coach arrived at the motel in a small vehicle with equipment crammed in the back seat. Kathie squeezed in with the gear and we were off to the pier.

Immediately, there was a sign of trouble. My coach, who I had just met, was shaking uncontrollably and having trouble holding onto the steering wheel. Was he drunk? What have I paid for here? It turned out that earlier in the morning, he swam from Alcatraz to the mainland without a wet suit. Having made this swim many times before he expected to tremble for some time. I would be wearing a wet suit, but it was unnerving to sit next to a guy who was shaking from the cold water I would be soon be swimming in.

For 24 hours, I had been falling into a negative mindset focused on things I could not control. I focused on the coldness of the water, the wind, the size of the waves and the coach's shivering. As a result, I created needless anxiety which took away energy I needed to achieve my goal of completing the swim. I had to reframe of my thinking and I had to do it soon.

At the dock we met the captain of the boat. He greeted us in such a warm, friendly way it reduced some of my anxiety. He asked how I felt, and I told him I was nervous and hadn't slept. He asked, "Well, what's the worst thing that can happen?" He gave me a grin and answered his own question. "You could drown."

I laughed. His statement put into practice one of the therapeutic tools I have used to help clients confront their fears. Now he used it on me! It proved to be as helpful as I'd hoped. It brought some peace of mind to realize that whatever the worst case scenario would be, I could handle it - even death. The captain's words may have been a joke, but they reminded me that God was with me. And with God there is no catastrophe, there is no end of the world, there is only hope.

My faith gave me the peace I needed to finally reframe my thoughts, and I started to focus on the things I could control; my effort, swim technique, and attitude. I reminded myself that I was prepared. I had put in hours practicing my technique by swimming miles in the pool and open water. Instead of viewing the swim as a threat, I made the choice to see it as an opportunity to learn and improve. I told myself it was time to make the effort, get myself to the start line and face the challenge.

The boat arrived at Alcatraz, and as we bobbed with the waves, my coach pointed at a freighter anchored at the mainland. He told me to aim for it, as the current would drift my body near to the entrance into Aquatic Park. After a final good luck hug from Kathie, I jumped in the water and started swimming. My wet suit, booties and gloves helped with the initial submersion into the icy waters.

Alcatraz Island, just before the swim

With a new attitude, I focused on things I could control; my technique and staying pointed at the freighter. Soon, I was feeling more confident and in a rhythm.

About halfway into the swim I came to the turbulent wave pool area where four currents come together. As coach had warned me, I needed more muscle to pull through it. It was also at this point that I realized how cold the water was - my face felt like an ice cube. But I kept moving forward.

I continued to swim toward the freighter and amazingly, after an hour and half, the entrance to Aquatic Park was in front of me. Finally, I was in water shallow enough to touch bottom and I walked the remaining steps to shore. I felt triumphant as Kathie and my coach were there to greet me with towels, hugs and handshakes.

Cancer
Ultramarathon

After the hike in the Rockies, dark, threatening clouds moved in when a follow up PET Scan in October revealed four lesions of cancer had redeveloped in my bone and liver. The adventure trail twisted again. Devastated, I began to seriously wonder whether I'd ever beat this. The veil of hopelessness descended over my life and with it came anger: "Why in the hell didn't my immune system and treatment kill this damn shit for good?"

My family was crushed by the news. Kathie and I talked about our feelings and reminded each other that this was an up and down odyssey with no simple path to navigate. We took comfort in facing it together and trusted there would be a plan to deal with this stumbling block. We knew that new research and treatments were surfacing all the time. We were also grateful to have the best medical facility and the most determined oncologist and medical team working on our behalf.

By mid-autumn, my oncologist readjusted our plan and I had begun eight IV immunotherapy sessions of the drug "B" which caused me to cancel my plan to run the Madison Marathon. It was the second marathon cancellation due to cancer which further frustrated me.

Still, at the time my treatment began, news reports came out about former President Carter's miraculous remission of melanoma brain cancer using drug "B." It provided some hope in what has been a dark end of the year.

The immunotherapy sessions of drug "B" initially proved effective in shrinking the cancer lesions and, outside of irritating itching, side effects were minimal. I saw it as another blessing to be able to physically tolerate these medications.

But in April of 2016, a PET Scan revealed small advances of cancer. The oncology report indicated areas consistent with a relapse of my melanoma and suggested early evidence of drug "B" failure. It was yet another change in my recovery landscape which had already been marked by temporary highs and difficult setbacks. It was sinking in. What I once thought would be a 5K cancer run, then a marathon, had now become an ultramarathon.

Discouraged, my thoughts headed south. I wondered with each treatment failure if my options would soon run out. Kathie was also taken back by the news but together we looked to our tenacious trail guide to determine a new plan of attack. Since drug "A" worked well the first time, my oncologist decided to re-introduce a double dose of checkpoint inhibitor drugs, including drug "A" and drug "C." For four treatment sessions, three weeks apart, I began IV immunotherapy with both drugs in hope of energizing my immune system to destroy the intruding cancer cells.

Stay positive, I told myself, but it was easier said than done. Geez, I was a psychologist. I should know the tricks to keep my thoughts hopeful and upbeat. The reality however, was that I struggled with negativity.

This isn't uncommon as most of us have a tendency to focus on the negative. It is more a learned behavior than something in our genes but most of us have developed a habit to zone in on worry and catastrophe. The well-known brain researcher, Dr.Sood, sees the human mind as shortsighted, lacking self control and guided by rigid biases. It jumps to premature conclusions and frequently gets hijacked by impulses, infatuations and fear. Although a phenomenal tool, the mind falls prey to distractions and the sway of emotions (Sood 2013).

I wish I could say I maintained a positive outlook throughout this journey but the progression of my cancer cast a dark shadow. I drifted into periods of apathy and withdrawal. I didn't know what to say and it didn't seem worth the effort anyway. I found myself worrying about minor things and the smallest errands felt like major tasks. As a result, I was less patient, more easily annoyed, and, consequently, often irritated with Kathie. On top of all this, feelings of guilt would flood in making me unable to sleep in the early morning.

I did what I could to cope with these moods but sharing my feelings with Kathie was most helpful. She was my rock through this journey. I didn't need someone to fix the problem; I just needed someone who listened, and Kathie understood this. She wanted to know how I felt and since she was unable to read my mind, telling her was critical. Believing my periods of depression must show, I was surprised to learn how unaware she had been.

I clearly had work to do. My Scandinavian heritage taught me to withhold feelings. My work as a psychologist conditioned me to be the listener and rarely share. But we were on this adventure together and I needed to communicate. Initially, it felt risky and uncomfortable but it was worth the effort. Opening up to Kathie about my fears and times of depression helped reframe my thinking and improved my mood.

Sharing my feelings in a support group was another important resource. Expressing feelings and relating my story encouraged others to share as well. The clinic had a number of support groups specific to certain cancers (breast, prostate, lung, etc.). Unfortunately, although melanoma is the number one cancer in young adults ages 25 to 29 and one of the fastest growing cancers in the United States, there was no melanoma group. As a result, with help from my oncologist, research assistant Heidi, Kathie and I embarked on organizing a monthly support group in September 2016.

Despite the treatment and setbacks - and I still had a full time job - my training for the July 31st San Francisco Marathon was amazingly on target. I was running three to four days a week and by May had progressively increased my Sunday morning run to 16 miles.

My ability to stay on target was made easier by having Kevin Wentworth as my running partner. Like clockwork, every Saturday evening I'd get a text asking if I'd be at our 7:30 a.m. run the next day. He's run with me in the rain, subzero temperatures and stifling heat. Together we survived a cataclysmic deluge on a trail race in Copper Harbor, Michigan, and trudged through a near blizzard early one spring in central Minnesota. We have done countless 5 and 10K events, competed in marathons in Boston, Deadwood, Moab and Leadville, and ran the Grand Canyon Rim to Rim.

A quiet, deliberate mannered guy, Kevin is remarkably consistent and agreeable. He's somewhat shy, indecisive, a little cheap and will more likely go along with things, which has probably been one of the reasons we've been able to keep our running partnership together all these years. I'm compulsive and prefer a well-known run route, Kevin is willing to go along with any decisions I make about the run.

"Kevin, let's turn right here."

"Sure, OK."

"Kevin, let's run the 8-mile town route."

"Sure, OK."

"Kevin, we're going to run naked."

"Sure, OK."

I'm a runner who starts out too fast, forgets to pace and has trouble holding on in the latter stages. Kevin, on the other hand, starts out slowly and gains strength the farther he goes. I'm a runner who breathes heavily and my body shows the agony I'm enduring while Kevin has an easy going style which looks slow but is deceivingly fast. I prefer not to talk when running (usually it's because I simply can't) while Kevin is comfortable discussing life situations. He'll ask me questions and I respond with one word responses or grunts. How he's been able to put up with me all these years is astounding.

It's near impossible to accomplish anything alone in life, so I was extremely grateful to have the support of people like Kevin and others to prepare for the marathon. Having a dream to compete is one thing but turning dreams into reality requires having a plan and making the effort to execute it. When we encounter setbacks, we must rely on the people around us to keep our dream alive and the fire lit in order to keep moving forward. I was fighting cancer and had a dream to run the marathon. Trust me, I needed fire-lighters, not firefighters around me. I needed people to inspire me and help me draw away from doubt and negativity.

As the Fourth of July approached, I needed my firelighters when I hit a major setback. I had only two long runs to complete before tapering for the marathon. I awoke July 2nd at our cabin planning to accomplish one of the runs in the next two days but the strong cup of coffee I drank didn't seem to energize me. In fact, my head felt groggy, I was easily fatigued and needed rest after the most minor tasks. At one point during the day my family went out boating while I fell asleep in the cabin. Initially I thought my marathon training had caught up with me and rest would help, but when I crawled out of bed a few hours later, I didn't feel any better.

After a few days of this, I messaged my oncology team. I told them my energy was pathetic and fatigue had interfered with my training. I was supposed to run a marathon in four weeks but I was unable to walk across the room without taking a break; running was definitely out of the question. I also had the nagging thought, Will this be another cancelled marathon? The idea of was maddening. I needed this one.

On July 11 my oncologist responded back, "It sounds like the thyroid may be taking a hit." He added, "If you're not feeling well, do you want to come in to see me tomorrow? I'll see you anytime." I was grateful for his response to adjust his busy schedule - to know someone had my back was tremendously reassuring. His support eased my uneasiness so I decided to wait for our regularly scheduled appointment.

Lab results revealed that I've suffered from endocrine dysfunction due to adrenal and thyroid insufficiency. The 12 weeks of drug "A", 24 weeks of drug "B" and the 12 weeks of the combo drug cocktail of drugs "A" & "C" had taken its toll. Crap! Not good anytime but three weeks before a marathon? My trail guide started me on hydrocortisone replacement and a thyroid hormone.

I received more bad news when a PET Scan revealed the progression of cancer at two main sites, my liver and eighth right rib. Damn! It was another difficult bump in a series of disappointing setbacks and each one took a little more out of me. Like swimming in green soup, the murkiness of this journey upset the clarity and my sense of direction. Throughout this whole journey, I had said nothing about dying from melanoma because I never expected to, but for the first time I began to doubt.

My oncologist referred us to a specialist in Radiology Oncology for radiation therapy. He believed focal radiation treatments to the main sites could reduce the lesions and have a generalized effect to non-radiated cancer tissue. He also wanted an MRI of my head to rule out cancer metastasizing to my brain and scheduled it five days before the marathon. As Kathie and I left the clinic, we picked up the medication at the pharmacy and I began taking it immediately.

Incredibly, my energy was back the next day! The lack of training for 13 days, however, took its toll on my stamina. With only 17 days until the marathon I had work to do to get my 68-year-old body ready to run 26.2 miles. I knew long distances would not help so I decided to rebuild strength running short distances two to three times per week.

I also called my daughter Keri, who would run the marathon with me, to confer about our race strategy. She agreed to a plan of systematic running and walking. We decided to run the first four miles and then walk one minute. From then on, we would run one mile followed by walking one minute and we would continue this until we reached the finish. Our run pace would be comfortable and the walking pace brisk.

In mid-July, I saw the radiation oncologist and his nurse practitioner, and they explained an intricate preparation plan and treatment procedure to radiate the cancer from my liver and rib. I expressed my determination to run the San Francisco Marathon. The oncologist listened to me and said, "Even with cancer, one has to live life." His words struck what has been my working philosophy. I didn't want the negativity of a diagnosis to fill my life with bitterness, fear or anger. Cancer wasn't going to stop me from experiencing a life of purpose.

We scheduled the radiation sessions for after the marathon, but the preparation phase began immediately. Because the radiation beams have to strike the exact spot, I went through a CT/MRI set up which would assist the doctor in aiming the beams. To determine the exact location, I had to wear large goggles during the scan and periodically hold my breath. Holding my breath kept a colored bar I was viewing in a certain range. In a sense, it was practice. Later, during the actual radiation treatment, it would be necessary for me to hold my breath on a technician's command and keep the colored bar in the appropriate range. Holding my breath would also initiate the machine to fire treatment beams into me. My claustrophobia had not gone away, so none of this - being in a tube, wearing goggles, holding my breath - was easy. Thankfully, Kathie was in the scan room to provide distraction and reassurance.

A few days later, another specialist performed a procedure to further help my radiation oncologist locate the cancer. Guided by ultrasound, the radiologist slowly penetrated my body three times with a long needle down to my liver and left a gold marker. As I slid off the table, I thanked him for increasing my net worth!

After that, they did a scan of my brain to check for the spread of cancer. The MRI of my head was negative, but I told my kids it was positive for high parental intelligence. They didn't buy it.

Preparation done, it was finally time to focus on San Francisco, a family reunion and the marathon. I boarded the plane with Keri and Kathie feeling hopelessly inadequate to run 26.2 miles. Keri admitted she was not ready to run the distance either as she had only been running once a week and her longest was only seven miles. I felt somewhat comforted knowing we would be in it together, and we had our strategy of run a mile/walk a minute. Despite my doubts, I was determined to get myself to the start line whether I finished or not.

In the early morning, Keri and I lined up with thousands of other runners on the Embarcadero in San Francisco for the start. Side by side we ran through a vacated Fisherman's Wharf, then on to Chrissy Field and through the Presidio. We stuck to our plan running the first four miles then alternating walking a minute and running a mile. The weather was cool and cloudy and perfect. From the Presidio, we made our way onto the majestic Golden Gate Bridge with both of us feeling surprisingly strong. It was an out and back run with the tops of the Golden Gate shrouded in a maritime fog. Running with a mass of runners off to the side of the multilane bridge and above the waters of San Francisco Bay was epic.

From the bridge at mile 15.5 we entered Golden Gate Park with

its towering eucalyptus and redwood trees. After a long run over hilly roads, we left the park at mile 17 and passed crowds cheering the half marathoners who were completing their run.

At this point, the gap in my training began to show. With every stride my legs ached but my heart was filled with gratitude and respect for Keri's support. For both of us to be there together, regardless of our minimal training, was amazing. Keri and I encouraged one another as we ran through the Haight Asbury and the Mission District, but now I needed to run shorter distances and walk more than a minute. From the Mission District, we headed through an industrial area on our way to AT&T Park and the finish. With two miles to go I looked at my watch and estimated that perhaps we could make the finish in less than five hours! But my mind must have been half numb because my legs did not agree. As hard as I tried, the run distances continued to get shorter and walking time longer.

We stayed together past AT&T Park where the smell of hot dogs hung over the people lined up for a Giants baseball game. The last two miles seemed like a life span but finally Keri and I crossed the finish line feeling the mix of relief, joy and pride. We had finished a race that a week earlier seemed improbable.

It was a marathon adventure and like all the adventures, including my cancer journey, it required support and assistance from others. We failed to break five hours but it didn't matter. I was facing radiation and immunotherapy as soon as I returned home from San Francisco. What mattered was an oncology team that made it possible for me to be at the start line and a daughter who supported me to the finish.

Rim to Rim

Twenty years from now you will be more disappointed
by the things you didn't do than by the ones you did do.
So throw off the bowlines. Sail away from the safe harbor.
Catch the trade winds in your sail. Explore. Dream. Discover.
                                    - Mark Twain

It was an epic adventure when five of us ran 24 miles from the south rim of the Grand Canyon, down to the canyon floor, across the mighty Colorado River and finished on the north rim. You cannot see all the Grand Canyon in one view and it's impossible to adequately describe the grandeur of it. The power of rushing water over eons of time formed the canyon, but as we witnessed firsthand the morning sun illuminating the gorge, we surely saw the hands of God.

I end my athletic adventures with the Rim to Rim because it symbolized what my cancer journey has become; an unknown adventure with a series of twists and turns, triumphs and setbacks, ups and downs. The run through God's cathedral was challenging and carried with it risks similar to any adventure. And yet, through the elements of danger there was wonder and joy.

I t was 4:30 in the morning and still dark in the park. We unloaded the vehicles, hid the keys and made our way to the Bright Angel Trailhead. Our goal of running the Grand Canyon rim to rim was soon to begin. In relative silence, we made a final check of the gear, water and food we would need. The morning air was cool but given the forecast for high temperatures, we wanted to get moving.

Rim to rim runs/hikes are strongly discouraged by the National Park Service. Rescues are frequent as people either underestimate the difficulty of the trail, overestimate their abilities, or fail to consume enough water and food during the trek. The five of us knew this adventure wasn't going to be easy but we had trained for months to prepare ourselves. We could only hope it would be enough.

Our biggest concern was the heat. Temperatures in the lower canyon are typically more than 20 degrees warmer than on the rim, and many hikers each year suffer or die from heat related ailments. This is why most runners make these attempts in April or October when temperatures are moderate. We had chosen May 16, the day the National Park had officially opened. We had hoped the cool spring weather would last, but for the last few weeks it had been unseasonably warm.

As the five of us silently made our final adjustments, five elk bounded up from out of nowhere and stopped just twenty feet from us. For a few seconds in the surreal dimness we stared at the elk who were staring at us. As they bounded away, we wondered

Grand Canyon Rim to Rim Course

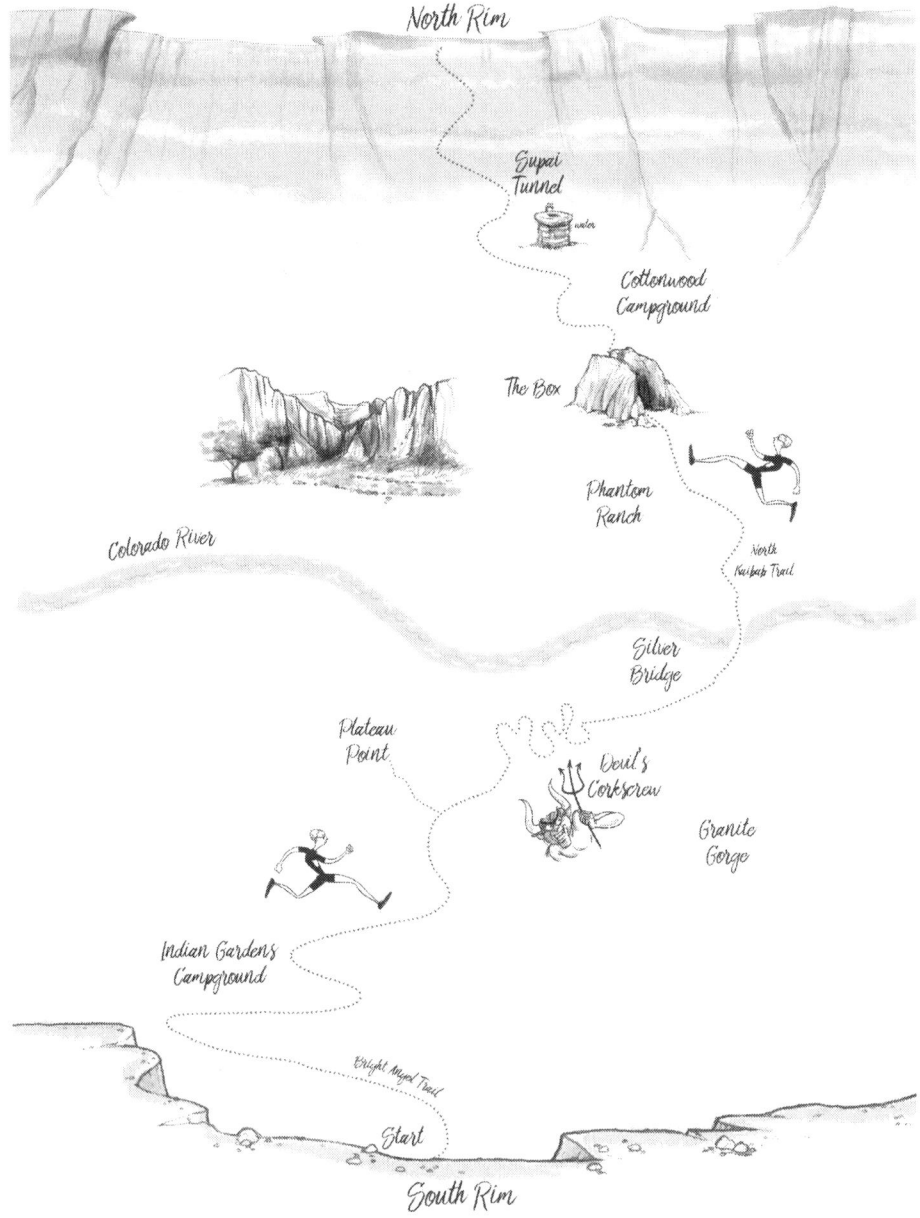

North Rim

Supai
Tunnel

water

Cottonwood
Campground

The Box

Colorado River

Phantom
Ranch

North
Kaibab Trail

Silver
Bridge

Plateau
Point

Devil's
Corkscrew

Granite
Gorge

Indian Gardens
Campground

Bright Angel Trail

Start

South Rim

if it was a Grand Canyon welcome or an unsettling omen. Either way, we needed to get going; the sun would soon be up.

It had been four years since Dave Roseen first approached me with the idea of running the Grand Canyon rim to rim. I was intrigued, but for a long time other things took center stage. The idea was never out of mind, however, so when Doug and Cyndi Smith of Red Wing and their adult children, Kristin and Katie, were planning to hike/run the canyon with a Phoenix Medical Group, it seemed like the right time. Soon, three other Red Wing runners, Josh Cichy, Keith Peterson and Kevin Wentworth, signed on. The plan was for Doug, Cyndi, Kristin and Katie to start on the North Rim and go to the South Rim while the five of us would be going south to north. The Smiths would leave a van for us at their end and we left two vehicles for them at ours.

We opted to take the longer Bright Angel Trail primarily because of the four water faucets which we hoped would sustain us to the Colorado River. The run covered 24 miles beginning at 6800 feet on the South Rim and then descending to 2400 feet at the river. After crossing the bridge over the river, we would reach Phantom Ranch at 9.9 miles and then ascend approximately 14 miles to 8240 feet at the North Rim. Altogether the elevation gain, including some ups and downs along the way, was about 6,000 feet.

Knowing it would be a significant challenge, I felt both an uneasiness and excitement. I wanted to get going, however, as running on the trail would quell some of the nervousness.

I plunged into the dark canyon running carefully to get my bearings through the numerous switchbacks. I lifted my feet and kept my eyes focused where they landed. To prevent erosion, the trail is maintained with logs and rocks periodically planted across the path. The sheer cliffs plunged to a seemingly bottomless abyss. To sightsee, it was critical to stop first and then look.

At one point looking into the vast black canyon, I spotted ant-like lights coming from a group of runners far below us. The sheer depth of our journey staggered me.

The morning sun entered the canyon with inspirational beams revealing the yellow, orange and golden brown of the canyon walls.

The Grand Canyon is a breathtaking sequence of rock layers that serve as a window into time with the carving of the canyon the most recent chapter in a long story. That long story includes rock nearly two billion years old at the bottom of the canyon, land masses colliding and drifting apart, mountains forming and eroding away, sea levels rising and falling and the relentless force of moving waters. Scientists estimate that it has taken three to six million years to cut the Grand Canyon into the world's most spectacular example of the power of erosion - a chasm 277 miles long, up to 18 miles wide and, on average, one mile deep.

As the sun rose, the trail became clearer and the shafts of heavenly light brought energy to my feet. Our pace quickened as we descended into the most famous canyon in the world. The downhill course pounded on my knees and calf muscles. I attempted to use gravity effectively but with switchbacks of the trail and the cliffs to one side, it required nearly constant braking to slow my pace. Approaching Indian Gardens Campground at mile 4.6, the trail wasn't as steep and became easier to run - although it was here we had our first fall. Keith, the most able runner of the group, bloodied his knee and smashed his camera.

Keith's fall was a reminder that bad things can happen without warning. I told myself not to become complacent and to focus on running the trail.

At this point, our group had already descended 3,000 feet and the temperature was rising. Passing the cutoff to Plateau Point we continued to descend into a series of long switchbacks called the Devil's Corkscrew. From there, we headed north in the direction of the Colorado River. As we plunged deeper into the gorge, it felt like it was swallowing us. A vague sense of foreboding settled in my gut. How deep were we going, and, more importantly, would we ever get out?

Through the Devil's Corkscrew with its surrounding buttes, the trail became more rugged and we passed a mountain goat off to our left. With each switchback, anticipation rose in catching our first view of the mighty Colorado. As the trail descended, the air filled with moisture until finally at the River Trail the brownish

blue water of the Colorado could be seen. At 2450 feet we headed east along a rolling trail above the rushing river. The views up
and down Granite Gorge were dramatic. Finally, we reached Silver
Bridge where we paused to take pictures and fuel up with food and
water.

The bridge swayed underneath us, somewhat unnerving with
the river roaring below. The power of the rapids took our breath
away. For a long moment, we stood above the cascading waterway

and listened to its roar. The river has shaped the canyon over the
last six million years and as the river cuts down, the canyon deep-
ens.

While it would have been pleasant to stay longer, we needed to
get going. Temperatures were rising and we still had more than
half the run to complete. The five of us exited the bridge, emerged
onto the Bright Angel Delta, and then followed the North Kaibab
Trail which headed toward Phantom Ranch. This consisted of a
number of rustic cabins accessible only by mule, foot or river raft.

As we approached the ranch, Kristin and Katie Smith appeared.
Seeing two familiar young women lifted our spirits until they told
us they ran the 14 miles in less time than we five able-bodied males
completed our ten. It humbled me as we left the ranch and made

me uneasy as the most challenging part of the run was ahead.

Running uphill we entered The Box, a massive 3.7 mile canyon that became a narrow, twisting hallway hemmed in by rock. The walls were enormous as we gradually traversed our way up alongside the Bright Angel Creek.

As the trail left the narrow confines of The Box, the uphill grind began to take a toll. With Cottonwood Campground a long four miles ahead with progressively steeper climbs, my pace slowed and my spirits dipped. We had ten miles to go, my legs were tired and the rest of the trail was basically uphill.

Keith Peterson running down the trail

Doug and Cyndi Smith, veterans of this hike, arrived on their way to Phantom Ranch. They looked to be in good shape, but later we heard that after crossing the river, Cyndi had serious problems with dehydration. She was a resilient woman and they would eventually finish, but this would lengthen their hike to 15 hours.

With the steady climb, I periodically resorted to power walking to relieve the ache in my legs. With the exception of Keith and Kevin, we all moved at a snail's pace. At one point, I broke into a run but Josh remarked that he was walking as fast as I was running. Although I was happy that he had enough energy left to speak, his comment hardly lifted my spirits.

After running 15.5 miles, we arrived at Cottonwood Campground. I put on a clean pair of dry socks, refueled with two Gu packets and a Little Debbie cherry pie. With water bottles filled we left the shaded campground and headed onto the exposed trail that twisted relentlessly upward. We had 4,240 vertical feet left to climb to the North Rim and it was hot! Temperatures were hovering near 100 degrees. After crossing a small creek, Dave and I soaked our shirts and exhilarated in squeezing the cold water over our heads.

Soon we reached Roaring Springs, a green oasis where we could resupply our water. Here several springs spout from the Muau limestone cliffs and supply water to both Grand Canyon rims. As I was preparing to leave, a group of runners from Hawaii told me that the next water stop at Supai Tunnel was just a short distance away. As a result, I only filled one of my water bottles.

The narrow trail grew steeper, switchbacks more numerous and it quickly became clear that having only one full bottle of water was a big mistake. I drained it early and it seemed like I'd never get to the tunnel and the water faucet. A lone hiker passed me coming down from the North Rim. I stopped her to ask how far it was to the tunnel, and she simply answered, "Far."

Negative thoughts entered my mind. I beat myself up for failing to fill both water bottles and taking someone's opinion of the distance. My legs hurt with each step and turn of the trail. I yearned to see the tunnel. I began to fear that this run would never end; that I was doomed to this climb eternally. But I tried to shake these thoughts off. Stay positive, I told myself, this too shall pass.

The shadeless and dusty climb zigzagged upward through the Esplanade sandstone via the tunnel, until finally we reached the confined, rocky draw at 6840 feet. I made a beeline to the faucet and drank, relishing the cold water soothing my parched lips and throat. Keith and Kevin had arrived earlier and it wasn't long before Josh and Dave wearily made their appearance. Depleted and out of gas, it was a relief to sit and rest.

But we couldn't rest forever. We were close to the top. I ascended the final mile passing through a forest of White Fir, Douglas Fir, ponderosa pine and aspen. In the forest, the trail began to level out and suddenly there it was, the North Kaibab Trailhead and the finish.

I made it to the North Rim, a little over 23 miles and 8 hours 35 minutes from the start. Keith was there to greet me and within a short time Kevin, Josh and Dave joined us. With high fives, we congratulated each other on our accomplishment and headed to the waiting van. We devoured the food Kristen had left for us, changed clothes and began the five-hour drive to the South Rim.

As the van drove away from the Grand Canyon, each of us had special moments to share with the others. We spoke of how drawn we were by the beauty of its colorful spheres and buttes. We told of the excitement and fear we felt descending farther into the canyon. We each had a unique awareness of the canyon's depth which caused an uneasiness and thoughts of not making it back out.

For me, having run out of water in the oppressive heat, there were moments when the finish was unknown. But I had been in similar situations and had learned that in order to finish something I needed to keep restarting again and again. Marred by strain, sweat and worry, sometimes the only thing to do was to keep going and trust the finish would come.

Keep on
Running

The day after we returned from San Francisco I was in the radiation department and began five days of treatment to zap the cancer out of my liver and 8th right rib. At the same time, my oncologist put me on a two-week treatment regime with the immunotherapy drug "C."

After the radiation sessions, PET Scans in September and December demonstrated the radiation treatments were effective in shrinking the lesions in my liver and eighth right rib and for a while, my immune system, in concert with drug "C," seemed to be keeping a lid on any new cancers.

In January however, another PET Scan revealed a new lesion on my gall bladder. My medical team discussed treatment strategies and eventually decided on a targeted drug therapy. This is a more standard chemo treatment where drugs are attacking the cancer directly.

On February 12, I began my new therapy at home in capsule form. A week into treatment, my body reacted with shaking chills, headache, fatigue and fever. My medical team instructed me to stop the medication immediately, although the side effects continued for several days.

Three days away from my 28th American Birkebeiner race, my body was too weak to finish 50 kilometers. Temperatures however, had been unusually warm and a recent rain removed much of the snow cover. It was a bittersweet godsend for me; two days later organizers cancelled the race.

The next day I received an unexpected call from Dr. M. He asked for an update on the recent side effects. After listening closely, he came up with a new plan, prescribing drug "D", an anti-inflammatory drug used to treat and prevent gout attacks and familial Mediterranean fever. After several days of this drug, they reintroduced the targeted drugs and within eight days of his call, I was back on the full dosage of the treatment; this time with no side effects.

I came to realize that Dr. M had the mental attitude of an elite athlete. He saw defeat as merely a small delay on the road to success. He had a belief in his ability to succeed and had a commitment to pursuing answers. His positive attitude was contagious and helped Kathie and I see problems as temporary challenges to overcome.

In addition, he seemed to view cancer as a chess match and was willing to obtain the expertise of colleagues to assist in the next move. In consultation with us, he sorted through the information and options genuinely willing to share decision making. This type of relationship, having information and control, yet with expert guidance, was tremendously appreciated.

On March 9, I had my 15th PET Scan followed by our consultation with Dr. M. As we experienced many times, anxiety rose as we anticipated the results of the tests.

We sat silently in the windowless room, fidgeting restlessly. Finally, Dr. M. appeared and as he walked in, I tried to read the expression on his face. Thankfully, he didn't leave us waiting long. After a quick greeting, he said, "Complete resolution, Dr. Asp! Complete resolution."

Kathie blurted out, "You're kidding!"

He grinned, but said, "I wouldn't kid with something like this." Just like the first time we met him, Kathie jumped out of the couch and hugged him.

Miracles do happen. I believe on this journey, through the triumphs and setbacks and the ups and downs, God has been alongside providing strength and support. Each day He showers blessings. I just need to keep my eyes open to see it. I just need to be aware of His presence and the powerful ways He demonstrates His love and grace.

Even with this good news, we still needed to trust Him. Kathie and I allowed ourselves to enjoy Dr. M's report and were extremely grateful, but we'd also been here before. We had lost our illusions. We knew some drugs work well initially, and then for unknown reasons, lose their effectiveness over time. Yet, we never lost hope.

I began this cancer adventure in May 2014 thinking it would be a short 5K run. I thought after a few tests and a couple of treatments, I'd be cured, and life would continue as it had. But the journey had taken unexpected turns. I developed prostate cancer, and the melanoma metastasized to stage four. Ultimately, the adventure turned into an ultra-marathon which had no mile markers and, at this point, no definitive finish. I also began this journey with significant claustrophobic fear of PET Scans and MRIs, but psychology does work! Now after repeated relaxation techniques and exposure to numerous tests, much of my anxiety has decreased.

To help cope with this cancer adventure, I've drawn on past athletic endeavors - many of which I've described in this book. While the places and events were exciting, it was the people I met who truly inspired me. My training partners, my competition and my supporters all brought a deeper meaning to the adventure and gave me strength to keep moving forward. There are simply too many to name, and they could never fully know the positive influence they have been on my life.

In a similar way, I have experienced extraordinary support on this cancer odyssey. From my medical team of doctors, nurses and technicians to people who sent cards, offered prayers and called to offer assistance, people showed up again and again when I needed them the most. I couldn't have coped without them.

Also, being a cancer patient has given me the honor to hear the stories of other cancer patients. Their stories of courage and determination have inspired me on my journey.

And, of course, throughout this adventure my wife, Kathie, my two children, Erik and Keri, and their significant others have been there to support me. Their love, presence and understanding has been invaluable. As it is when training for an Ironman, the more

I surround myself with people who keep the fire of hope lit, the better.

Often, after people have cancer they're not sure what to call themselves. Many don't like "patient" in that it implies sickness. Many people will call themselves a "survivor" from the moment they are diagnosed while others believe you have to be in remission for at least 5 years to use that label.

Arthur Frank, author of The Wounded Storyteller, describes himself after living with cancer as a "witness." Frank writes: "I have no quarrel with the notion of survivors, but my first choice as a designation is witness. Survival does not include any particular responsibility other than continuing to survive. Becoming a witness assumes a responsibility for telling what happened. The witness offers testimony to a truth that is generally unrecognized or suppressed. People who tell stories of illness are witnesses, turning illness into a moral responsibility" (Frank 1995).

"Human beings are God's language," Kushner tells us. This is particularly true when people find the courage and strength to ease the burdens of others. Every person who has cancer, a chronic disease or is struggling with an emotional/mental condition has a unique story waiting to be told. Everyone's experience is different, yet when we hear stories of others it facilitates our own awareness, reminds us we're not alone and reassures us of our normalcy. People help others through telling their story of suffering. Stories told between people offer a connection and an experience of empowerment.

Equally important, stories express truth and clear up misconceptions. When witnesses gives their testimony, fear of the C word can be rolled away and the stigmas of depression or mental illness can finally cease. The ugly face of victimization, with its dark clouds of secrecy, guilt and shame can be shattered. When we share our stories, new perspectives can be reached and the bonds of negativity can be released.

This can be difficult. It requires an acknowledgement of our weakness. It demands vulnerability. This is hard, and I have to continue to work on expressing my feelings because vulnerability is not a weakness, but a strength. It allows relationships to be more meaningful and increases the potential for a rewarding life.

My hope is that we, as humans, will not allow whatever suffering we might experience to interfere with our ability to live a meaningful life. My hope is we will not let anger, fear or the conspiracy of silence cloud our path and negate our choices. Instead, despite any repeated setbacks we may face on our journey, my hope is we will continue to get ourselves back to the start line again and again.

On a back hallway on the 10th floor of the clinic there is a framed letter written by a young physician named Dr. Tan. He was a Mayo Clinic resident and Hematology-Oncology Fellow who died from cancer at 33 years of age. His words are relevant for whatever suffering we may face.

"My personal thoughts are that if we as cancer patients are able to overcome the negativity of a cancer diagnosis, and continue to live and for some even die, with grace and dignity we will have already won the victory against cancer. Some journeys with cancer will be longer and others short, but what matters most is how we walk the journey. That journey need not be filled with angst, bitterness, why me questions, denial, rage, depression or even in some cases, an unrealistic pursuit of a long life. We should not allow fear of the dreaded C words to dictate how we live our lives. Rather that journey, no matter how long or short, can be a path filled with courage, acceptance, love, hope, faith, peace, joy, fellowship, serenity, a sense of purpose, grace and dignity.

"We and our loved ones did not choose to be afflicted with cancer, but we have a choice of how we deal and cope with this difficult diagnosis. I pray that God will grant us the courage to choose our paths wisely, the hope to live a purposeful life and the inner strength to live and die with dignity."

- Tow Shung Tan M.D. C.M.
November 6th, 1978 - May 17th, 2011

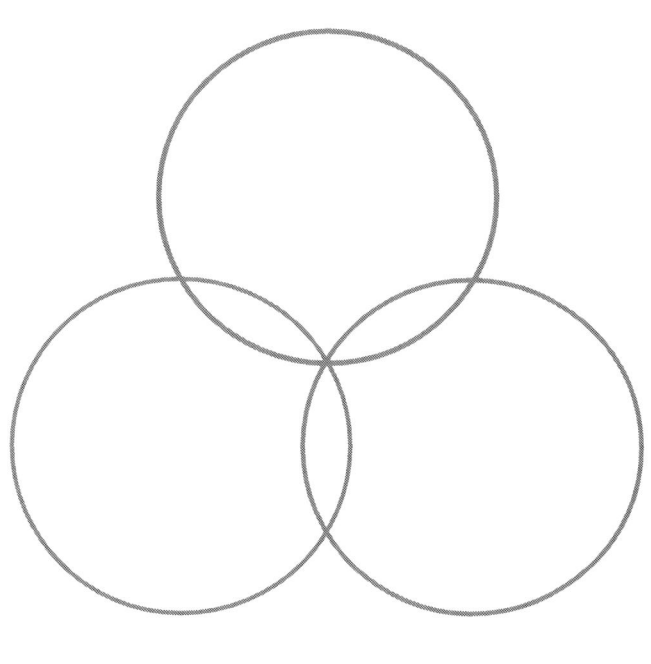

Resources

References

Dweck, C.S. (2006). <u>Mindset: The New Psychology of Success.</u> New York. Ballentine.

Frank, A.W. (2013). <u>The Wounded StoryTeller.</u> Chicago. University of Chicago Press

Gladwell, M. (2013). <u>David And Goliath</u>. New York. Back Bay

Kushner, H.S. (1981). <u>When Bad Things Happen To Good People.</u> New York. Anchor.

Meichenbaum, D. (2012). <u>Roadmap To Resilience: A Guide for Military, Trauma Victims and Their Families</u>, Clearwater, Fl. Institute Press

Sood, A. (2013). <u>The Mayo Clinic: Guide to Stress Free Living</u>. Boston. Da Capo.

Melanoma Fact Sheet
Melanoma Research Foundation
Washington D.C.
www.melanoma.org

ONE
Melanoma is one of the fastest growing cancers
in the U.S. and worldwide.

TWO
Every hour of every day one American dies from melanoma.

THREE
In ages 15-29, melanoma is the second most commonly
diagnosed cancer.

FOUR
Melanoma is the number one cancer in young adults 25-29.

FIVE
Melanoma is the leading cause of cancer death
in women ages 25-30 and the second leading cause
of cancer death in women ages 30-35.

SIX
The incidence of people under 30 developing melanoma
is increasing faster than any other demographic group,
soaring by 50% in women since 1980.

SEVEN
It takes only one blistering sunburn, especially at a young age,
to more than double a person's chance of developing
melanoma later in life.

EIGHT
Exposure to tanning beds before age 30 increases
a person's risk of developing melanoma by 75%.

NINE
Young people who regularly use tanning beds are 8 times more
likely to develop melanoma than people
who have never used them.

TEN
The World Health Organization's international
Agency for Research on Cancer (IARC) classifies tanning devices
into the highest cancer risk category-carcinogenic to humans.

ELEVEN
Melanoma does not discriminate by age, gender or race.
Everyone is at risk.

TWELVE
The lifetime risk of getting melanoma is about 1 in 50
for Caucasians, 1 in 1000 for African Americans
and 1 in 200 for Hispanics.

THIRTEEN
Melanoma is not just a skin cancer. It can develop anywhere
on the body, eyes, scalp, nails, feet, mouth, etc.

FOURTEEN
Nearly 90% of melanomas are thought to be caused by exposure
to UV light and sunlight.

Sun Protection Tips and Facts

Mayo Clinic Health System
Mayo Foundation for Medical Education and Research
2012
mayoclinichealthsystem.org

ONE
Avoid being out in the sun between 10 a.m. and 4 p.m.

TWO
Sun exposure on a cloudy day is only decreased by 30%.

THREE
Sand, snow, concrete and water can reflect the sun's rays
and increase the amount of sun exposure to your skin.

FOUR
Seek shade whenever possible.

FIVE
Apply sunscreen (recommended SPF of at least 30 and broad
spectrum) before going out and reapply every two hours,
more if sweating heavily or in the water.

SIX
Wear a wide brimmed hat and tightly woven clothing
with long sleeves and pants.

SEVEN
Keep children out of the sun entirely until 6 months old
(when it is safe to apply sunscreen).

EIGHT
Wear 100% UV-blocking eyeglasses.

NINE
Certain medications and antibiotics can make your skin
more sun sensitive.

TEN
Check your body monthly from head to toe for any new bumps
or moles.

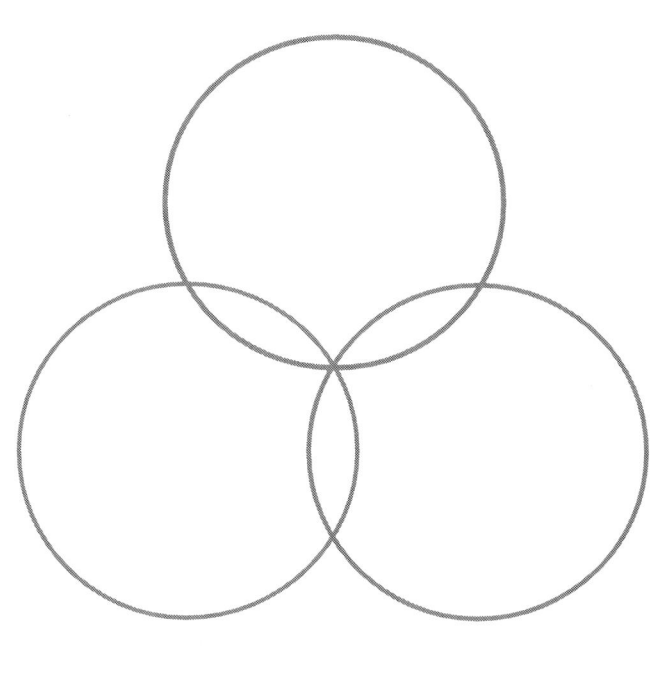

Coyote Dave
and
the Bobcats

Whatever challenges we face in life, it's important to live life with a sense of thankfulness, purpose and adventure. While risky, doing something out of the ordinary creates enriching experiences in our lives. Coyote Dave and The BobCats was one of those "wild and crazy" ideas that did just that.

Coyote Dave and the BobCats began years ago when I made a list of life goals I wanted to accomplish. One of those was to "learn how to play the guitar." After purchasing a guitar, I took three or four lessons, practiced and was able to play a few simple chords. At the same time, my running buddy, Kevin Wentworth, was also learning how to play. I decided I would know I had reached my goal by playing music in some type of public venue. I'm not a singer and knew nothing about writing songs, but I liked the "singer, song writer" title. It had a nice ring to it and seemed to flow from my lips...singer, song writer...singer, songwriter.

The evening before the American Birkebeiner Ski race, the public radio station, WOJB 88.9FM, plays Birkie theme music. Music written, sung and played by amateurs that celebrate the ski race happening the next day. What better venue to demonstrate that I reached my goal?

"Going To Hayward" was the result of writing a song, putting it to chords and singing it. After practicing it a few times, I approached Kevin with the idea of accompanying me on guitar, recording it and offering it to the radio station for Birkie music night. Kevin was sheepishly reluctant but the more beer we consumed, the braver he became and finally agreed. Naming ourselves Coyote Dave and the BobCats, we recorded the performance in my basement and submitted it to the station.

Sure enough, they accepted "Going To Hayward" and routinely play it during Birkie Week. The song also made the station's Gold 2016 Birkebeiner CD which is a compilation of 13 Birkie tunes regularly played on the station.

About the Author

 Dr. David Asp lives in Red Wing, Minnesota with Kathie, his wife of 43 years. They have two adult children.

He has been a psychologist for over forty years and currently practices at Mayo Health Services in Red Wing, Minnesota. As a cognitive behavioral psychologist Dr. David Asp has assisted patients in developing strategies to feel empowered and make desired changes. He has also worked with athletes of all ages and abilities in mental toughness and performance enhancement.

He has completed 16 marathons, 27 American Birkebeiner cross country ski races and is a three time Ironman finisher.

He has stage four melanoma cancer, but despite the challenges of cancer and treatment he continues to be active and live life.

This is his first book.

Made in the USA
Columbia, SC
11 February 2018